VANISHING CORNWALL

Merry Christmas, Mom!

love, mike
81

Daphne du Maurier

VANISHING CORNWALL

PHOTOGRAPHS BY CHRISTIAN BROWNING

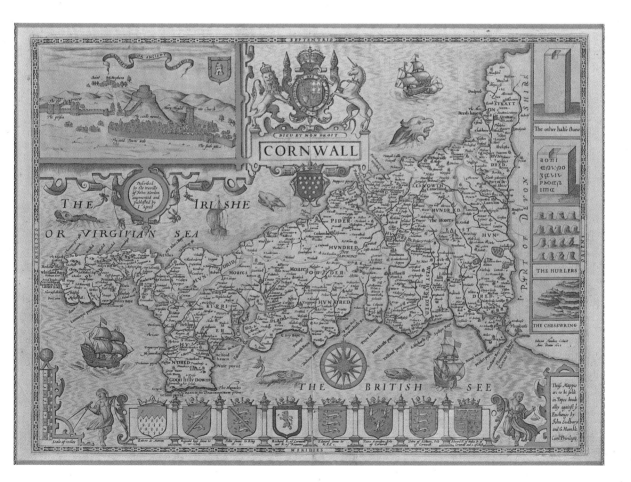

DOUBLEDAY & COMPANY, INC.
GARDEN CITY, N Y · 1981

First published 1967
This edition published 1981

ISBN 0-385-17832-8

Photoset in Great Britain by
Rowland Phototypesetting Limited
Bury St Edmunds, Suffolk
and printed and bound in Spain by
Grafichromo, S.A.- Córdoba

To the memory of my husband, because
of memories shared and a mutual love
for Cornwall; and to our son Christian,
who photographed the present, while I
rambled on about the past.

MENABILLY, 1966.

Contents

Prologue

I saw him thrash about in the long grass with a stick, and suddenly he thrust downwards with his hand and drew forth the wriggling form.

The women who were gathered round the back-door screamed. "Kill him quick," they shouted, "now, now, before he bites."

The gardener smiled, the snake held fast in his left hand, its head powerless. The darting tongue flickered and withdrew. He struck at the tail end with his stick once or twice, and the snake coiled. Then the gardener walked towards the big tree with the spreading branches that stood close to the back-door, a few yards away from the kitchen-garden.

"He'll not die yet," he told them, "he'll die at sundown."

He put down his stick and went to the tool-shed near by, coming back with a hammer and nail. The women watched him, fascinated. Then he drove the nail through the snake, somewhere between head and tail, and hammered it fast to the tree. He stood back and watched it writhe.

"He'll do that through the day," he observed, "but the venom will go out of him when the sun goes down. Then he'll die."

He turned, and went into the kitchen-garden. The women dispersed indoors, the scullery-maid chatting excitedly to the cook, the housemaid running up the back-stairs to tell the nurse. The drama was over. The normal routine of the day resumed its course. It was morning.

There was no one but myself now by the tree, and I drew nearer and stared up at the snake. It was not very big, nothing like the size of the monsters in the Zoo. The colour was greenish-black. The body swirled now and again, but not all the time. I wondered why it had to wait until long after tea to die. Perplexed, I moved away from the tree and went over to the wall near the downstairs nursery window. There was a table by the window and on it stood a cage, with the two doves inside. The doves had been given to me for my birthday. I was five years old. I stared at the doves as I had stared at the snake, and my feelings were mixed. Boredom was not a word as yet in my vocabulary, but, had I known it, it would have expressed what I felt. The doves bored me. They sat together on the perch, cooing or plucking at their feathers, and made a disgusting mess on the sanded floor of the cage. Every day they had to be given fresh sand, fresh drinking-water, fresh seed, and this took up valuable time that could be spent elsewhere, roaming the garden. My elder sister kept canaries, happy birds that trilled and sang, rocking themselves backwards and forwards on a little swing. She did not find the care of them irksome, but sang with them as she cleaned their cage. The doves were different. They huddled side by side, dispirited yet at the same time swollen with a sort of desperate greed, so that when they were fed they edged one another away from the small eating-trough, beaks darting, jabbing.

I went once more to stare at the snake upon the tree. He was moving still, the impotent tail struggling for release. He had not given up hope, and would not do so until the sun went down. He did not know that he was doomed to die. He was brave, because he was wild. He had never been caged. I ran quickly to the waiting doves, as yet unfed, slid back the rod that kept the fastening closed and opened the cage door wide . . .

Doves and snake were forgotten during the long summer's day. The farmer and his men were cutting hay in the nearby fields and my sister, eight years old, loved the handsome dark one, Arthur. He mounted her upon his horse and she smiled down at me, proud as a queen. The older man, Tom, swung me up upon his saddle. It was not the same, though. I had come off second-best.

They called us from the house to tea, and instead of having it out of doors we went to the stuffy nursery, for our nurse's aunt had travelled down from London to spend the day and everything must be just so. I remembered the doves, and stole a look out of the window. My heart jumped. Only one of them had gone, and his companion drooped alone upon the perch. This was terrible.

We sat ourselves to tea, my elder sister filled with dreams of Arthur, and the youngest, still in a high-chair, put out an imperious hand for jam on her buttered bread. Our elders talked. They had not discovered the open cage. The conversation droned on and on but I had no appetite, for somewhere the bolder dove was free, already meeting his wild fellows in the trees on Bookham Common, while his timid mate awaited his return.

"And what are the plans for August?" asked the visitor.

Our nurse, with a glance at her three charges, stirred her tea. "There's to be a change this year," she said, "something different. They are going to Cornwall."

The effect was dramatic, her emphasis on the word Cornwall intense. It sounded like a journey to the moon. I looked from her kind, grave face – for she was not smiling – to the visitor, who paused in surprise, a piece of cake midway to her mouth.

"To Cornwall?" she exclaimed.

They exchanged adult glances. Something unspoken seemed to be in the air. Silence fell, then they passed to other things, as though, for this moment, the subject was forbidden. I began to think again about the dove who had got away. Not for nothing had I named him Peter and his reluctant mate Wendy. He had been the first to go because some Never-Never-Land lay beyond Bookham Common; it could be that he was even now winging his way to Cornwall. Somehow the other one must follow him. Guilt was heavy upon me. Nobody must know. Another silence came, and looking about me I perceived that the nursery was in shadow and there was no longer a pathway of sun from the hall beyond. It would soon be sundown. Time for the snake to die.

I moved restlessly in my chair, and our nurse, with some possible intuition, searched my eyes. Once again she stirred her tea, but her eyes never left my face.

"Yes," she said slowly, "yes, they're going to Cornwall . . ."

I asked if I could get down and she nodded silently. I slipped from the room and ran outside to the doves' cage. A miracle had happened. The cage was empty. I looked up into the trees around, but nothing was there. Both birds had flown. Tomorrow would come recriminations, reproaches, scoldings for carelessness. It did not matter. The doves were free and so was I, for I would not have to feed them any more, or clean their cage.

A flickering streak of sunlight caught the higher branches of the big tree by the back door. I watched it fade away. Then I went up to the tree and saw that the long dark form no longer wriggled. The snake was dead.

The railway carriage was full. Our mother was with us, and a new nurse. A nursemaid, too, and a holiday governess. Truly all had changed, and there were a lot of people to care for three small children.

The train drew in to a bustling station. There was confusion, shouting. All of us were tired. Then, to enliven us, our mother said: "When we leave Plymouth we shall come to a bridge, and once the bridge is crossed we shall be in Cornwall."

We jumped about, excited. All was anticipation, and it was unbearable to wait. The adults smiled mysteriously. The train drew out of the station at last, and soon after there was a strange rattling sound as the carriage wheels ran upon the bridge. The governess, whipping up our fever, held up a warning hand. "Shut your eyes, quick," she commanded, "and keep them shut until we come to Cornwall."

We obeyed, but, cheating, I opened mine while we were still on the bridge. There was nothing to see, only chinks of water between what seemed to be iron bars, and the rattle of the train made a frightening sound. One moment there was light, the next darkness, then light, then darkness again. I was bewildered, and the few moments seemed like hours. Suddenly the rattle ceased, and the wheels changed their tune. Everything was light, and the sun streamed through the carriage window.

"There. Now we're in Cornwall," said our mother, laughing.

12

I stared out, disenchanted. For what was different about this? The country was just the same. There were houses on a hill, and another smaller station, even people and porters on the platform. What had I expected?

Everyone started talking. The new nurse fumbled with a picnic-basket. Cups of milk were given us, sandwiches, buns. Something tremendous was supposed to have happened, by passing from Devonshire into Cornwall.

Greatly deceived, I went on staring out of the window. There must be a mistake. Somewhere there awaited the hidden land. It was not this.

Five years old, and Mullion Cove . . . Ten years old, and Kennack sands . . . Nineteen years old, and the first sight of Fowey harbour . . . The children who had twice before crossed the Tamar bridge to Cornwall had now grown up, though the youngest was a schoolgirl still.

We were all ready for adventure, but the cage imprisoned us. The cage, indeed, was all we knew. Ours was the sanded floor, the seed, the water, even the rod on which to perch, the swing to make us gay. We were cherished, loved, protected. No trio of turtle-doves could wish for more.

The hired car swept round the curve of the hill, and suddenly the full expanse of Fowey harbour was spread beneath us. The contrast between this sheet of wide water, the nearby jetties, the moored ships, the grey roofs of Fowey across the way, the clustering cottages of Polruan on the opposite hill by the harbour mouth, and narrow, claustrophobic Looe where we had spent the night was astonishing, like the gateway to another world. My spirits soared.

The hired car deposited our mother and ourselves at the foot of the hill, by the ferry. We could either cross the ferry to Fowey or lunch first at the Ferry Inn here at Bodinnick. It was nearly one o'clock, and we chose the latter course. Before climbing the hill to lunch our eyes were caught by a board saying "For Sale" on a gate just above the ferry. Behind the gate was a rough piece of ground and a house by the water's edge, a strange-looking house, built like a Swiss chalet.

"Yes," said the ferryman standing near by, "they call it Swiss Cottage. They used to build boats there, down under, and have the second floor for lofts. The top floor was for living. It's for sale right enough."

We went to the Inn for lunch and afterwards, during coffee, our mother talked with the proprietor, enquiring first about lodgings on the opposite side in Fowey. We were touring Cornwall, she explained, with the idea of looking for a house for the holidays; we came from Hampstead, London.

I was too impatient to wait for the conversation to drag on. I jerked my head to the others to follow me, leaving my mother talking. We went down the hill. My sisters tried the gate by the ferry and went into the yard. I found another gate, and a pathway leading to the other side of the house. Here there was a garden, or what went for a garden, terraced uphill tier upon tier, and the chalet part of the house thrust itself forward, built, so it seemed, against the rock, with the windows facing straight out across the harbour. I went and stood beneath the chalet, the water immediately beneath me, and looked towards the harbour mouth. There were small boats everywhere, and yachts at anchor, but more stirring still a big ship was drawing near, with two attendant tugs, to moor a few cables' length from the house itself.

There was a smell in the air of tar and rope and rusted chain, a smell of tidal water. Down harbour, around the point, was the open sea. Here was the freedom I desired, long sought-for, not yet known. Freedom to write, to walk, to wander, freedom to climb hills, to pull a boat, to be alone. It could not be mere chance that brought us to the ferry, and the bottom of Bodinnick hill, and so to the board upon the gate beyond that said For Sale. I remembered a line from a forgotten book, where a lover looks for the first time upon his chosen one: "I for this, and this for me." The cage was not fastened, and of the three doves I should be the first to fly. The way was open.

Memories crowd in thick and fast. Learning to row, to scull, to snare a rabbit and gut a fish. Climbing upon the rotting hulls of abandoned ships. Bathing naked in deserted coves. Trespassing upon estates, even breaking in through shuttered windows, my mongrel sheep-dog at my heels. "Isn't it time you came back to London? We can't think what you find to do with yourself in Cornwall. Mummy and Daddy miss you dreadfully." A gentle hint from my aunt and god-mother, zealous in her devotion to a united family. It was she who gave me the doves when I was five. The woody tang of a campfire. The seepy tread of a moorland bog. The tall chimneys of Jamaica Inn. The splendid solitude of a grey manor house set deep amongst tall trees and rhododendrons growing wild, its owner ever absent from his home. Perhaps if I won a sweepstake I might live there. Menabilly . . . Menabilly . . . Manderley . . .

> "On the road to Mandalay,
> Where the flyin'-fishes play . . ."

Realization was a long way off. The hatch-way window looking over Fowey harbour was still my solace, and then a passing motor-cruiser with a handsome stranger at the wheel, who waved a hand in greeting, and later, with a soldier's cunning, made an assignation with me after dark. Some months afterwards, on my wedding-day, I looked out of the same hatch-way window at eight in the morning, and saw that the houses opposite had put out flags to greet the bride who went to church by water, and set forth to the harbour mouth for her honeymoon, bound for Helford River and Frenchman's Creek, in the motor-cruiser that had been her trysting-place.

Other craft we owned later, but this was his first love, *Ygdrasil*, named for the ash-tree of Norse mythology under which the gods held daily council. Year after year new engines would be installed and then ripped out, in his fervent belief that she would surmount the highest seas and plane above them to the far horizon. Stolid, enduring, she never went faster than seven knots. Some four-and-thirty years have passed, and now she lies facing seaward across the fields from Menabilly, high and dry for grandchildren to play in. Built in Nottingham, she cruised south-west to Cornish waters, and like her owner found content. Neither soldiering, nor the wars for which

15

soldiers are trained and which they must one day fight, dulled his passion for the sea.

His profession took us often from the Cornwall that we loved, but always we returned for leave and holiday. Once, fired with romantic ardour and heaven knows what boyish dreams of Cavalier and Roundhead, he brought his battalion of Grenadiers down to Fowey, and set them fighting on the Gribbin peninsula. The company commander, briefed to attack the Gribbin, lost himself and his men hopelessly in Menabilly woods and retired discomfited, the objective unachieved. Today the company commander is a major-general, and if I have done him less than credit doubtless he will correct me in his memoirs.

Real war came, disrupting life and leisure, and in the midst of it, and forever after, Cornwall became our true home. Bombs might fall on Plymouth, shaking the windows, mines explode above Pridmouth beach, Fowey and its harbour be given up to the American Navy planning for D-Day, but here at Menabilly the children grew and thrived. Now, like my caged doves of long ago, they have spread their wings and flown. The door was open. We had no belief in bars.

Memories are precious things, and whether good or ill are never sad. A country known and loved in all its moods becomes woven into the pattern of life, something to be shared, to be made plain. Those born and bred in Cornwall must have the greatest understanding of its people and their ways, its history and its legends, its potentiality for future growth. As one who sought to know it long ago, at five years old, in quest of freedom, and later put down roots and found content, I have come a small way on the path. The beauty and the mystery beckon still.

Chapter One

ORIGINS AND APPROACHES

CORNWALL projects from the body of England much as Italy falls from the land mass of central Europe. The two peninsulas, so dissimilar in size, are curiously alike in shape; both long, narrow, terminating in a pincer movement – the claw of Cornwall probing the grey Atlantic, while Italy's high-heeled boot, more delicately formed, treads the Ionian sea. Resemblance goes further, for each has a river in the north, spanning its breadth and flowing eastward: the Italian Po rising in Monte Viso near the French frontier and coursing to the Adriatic, the Cornish Tamar, its source close to the Devon border, making a natural boundary between Cornwall and Devon for fifty-seven and a half miles before it enters the English Channel.

The analogy might be pushed to its limit, comparing Italy's vertebrae, the central Apennines, with Cornwall's backbone, that high hinterland running from north to south, comprising Bodmin moor, the uplands of St. Breock and the startling perimeter of the china-clay district dominating Hensbarrow downs, where the white soil heaps thrust skyward, a mountain range in miniature. This said, the parallels can be dismissed, the map of Europe folded, and Italy, birthplace of the Roman Empire, cradle of the Renaissance, centre of art and learning throughout the centuries, culminating today in a new brilliance of industrial achievement and design, be left to her immortality.

Cornwall, little known, of small significance, remains the tail of England, still aloof and rather splendidly detached from the activity across Tamar hailed as progress; yet aware, despite her seeming isolation, that in those distant ages when Britons beyond the river

Cornwall remains the tail of England, still aloof and rather splendidly detached.

were tilling the soil and grazing cattle, the first settlers near the Land's End were already streaming tin, trading their mineral wealth with successive immigrants from Iberia and the Mediterranean lands to the east, and so glimpsing a civilisation hitherto unknown, ancient, wondrous, secreting amidst the Cornish soil the golden crescents and the blue beads of Crete.

This is no flight of fancy; these things have been found in the barrow graves of Cornwall. Who brought them from their places of origin, what venturers from the Aegean and the Mirtoon seas, braving the Atlantic Ocean in ships undaunted by the rugged coasts of Brittany and Ireland, to find haven at long last in Cornwall's river

Hayle, cannot be known with certainty. They are said to have been short and dark – but so were the later Celtic immigrants from France. Romantics of the nineteenth century and our own time, seeking an explanation for a black-haired beauty down Camborne way, or a dark-eyed fisherman casting his nets with easy grace from a vessel in Mount's Bay, would insist – and this was believed by the Cornish themselves – that men and women with such foreign looks must be descended from those unfortunate sailors who had been cast away upon the Cornish beaches when the Spanish Armada was defeated in 1588. If so, the Spanish sailors had a genius for begetting, reproducing themselves a thousandfold. It is more logical, and exciting, to go back to some 1400 years B.C. and remember earlier dark-eyed seamen, with narrow waists and braided hair, whose brothers, back in Knossos, may have leapt the Cretan bull.

There is in the Cornish character, smouldering beneath the surface, ever ready to ignite, a fiery independence, a stubborn pride. How much of this is due to centuries of isolation after the Roman conquest of Britain, when Mediterranean trade no longer found its way to south-western estuaries but went direct from Roman France to the eastern channel ports, and how much to the legacy of those dark-haired invaders with their blue beads and their circlets of gold, heirs of a civilisation existing long before Rome was even named, is something the Cornish can argue for themselves. As an outsider, with Breton forebears, I like to think that the two races, facing an Atlantic seaboard blown by identical gales, washed by the same driving mists, share a common ancestry, along with the Irish further west.

Superstition flows in the blood of all three peoples. Rocks and stones, hills and valleys, bear the imprint of men who long ago buried their dead beneath great chambered tombs and worshipped the earth goddess. Nowhere else in England do these symbols of eastern ritual stand, but here in Cornwall the tombs are with us still. Great slabs of granite, weather-pitted, worn, with another mighty slab, tip-tilted, to form a roof; these were the burial places of priests, perhaps of queens. Set in the high places, amidst scrub and gorse, the treasures they once contained long rifled by barbarians and the bones scattered, they stand as memorials to a forgotten way of life and a once-living cult. Sometimes today the setting is incongruous – a small field, perhaps, with a line of bungalows near by. Yet age has not destroyed their majestic beauty, nor plough and tractor tumbled the foundations. The stones, like the natural granite cast up from the earth by nature, defy the centuries. To stand beside them, whether on the heights of West Penwith, amongst the bracken of Helman Tor or in the little field above St. Cleer, is to become, as it were, an astronaut in time. The present vanishes, centuries dissolve, the mocking course of history with all its triumphs and defeats is blotted out. Here in the lichened stone is the essence of memory itself. Whether it was priest or chieftain, queen or priestess, who lay here once, prepared with solemn rites for the passage to the underworld, belief in immortality was theirs, Man's answers, from the beginning, to the challenge of death.

These, then, were the first tombs of Cornwall; but scattered throughout the length and breadth of the peninsula are other stones and other chambers, barrows and trenches, mounds and circles, so that it might be said that death, like the sea, is ever present. There is always a reminder, on some ridge or hillside, half-concealed perhaps by thorn or bracken, that stillness waits.

Later generations, with the guilt engendered by Puritan or Methodist upbringing, thought all standing or leaning stones were persons frozen by the merciless hand of God for dancing on a Sunday. Or so at least they told their children, though perhaps they knew better. For although, in those early days, they might not connect death and burial with the mounds and the old tilted stones in field and furze, they sensed that the place held magic, and whatever dwelt there under a brooding sky should be placated. Instinct, infallible, bade them place a hand upon the mound or stone, and spit. If the stone had a hole in it, like the Mên-an-Tol near Lanyon, the wisest thing to do was to crawl through it nine times against the sun. To crawl against the sun "backened" disease. The isolation that kept

If the stone had a hole in it, like the Mên-an-Tol, the wisest thing to do was to crawl through it nine times against the sun.

Cornwall from the rest of England thus preserved an ancient lore, an intuitive perception of things past.

The underworld that promised immortality held its treasures too, so that Cornishmen, from the beginning, have always dug for wealth. They were, are, tinners, copper-seekers, quarriers, slate-breakers, clay-workers, farmers; an earthy people with an earthy knowledge, the word earthy used not as a slight but as a salutation.

Those who desire to understand the Cornish, and their country, must use their imagination and travel back in time.

The right way to approach Cornwall is from the sea, sailing from southern Ireland to the Hayle estuary, as the first traders did in those

A Cornish farmer.

Crouching amongst the sand dunes and the tufted grass.

centuries B.C. – and surely with the same shock of surprise and relief, after a stormy passage, with the prevailing sou'westerly wind veering between the quarter and hard astern, to find that the inhospitable rock-bound Cornish claw thrusting into the Atlantic in quest of victims has, to the immediate north-west of its scaly hump, a welcome haven. Then, as today, the contrast was profound between the forbidding grandeur of the coast-line about Land's End, with its hinterland of granite tors, and the sudden emergence of St. Ives Bay, an encircling arm protecting the shallows and the yellow sands and the estuary of Hayle; but then, unlike today, the river, broad and deep, was tidal inland for four miles or more, cutting nearly to Mount's Bay on the south coast. Hayle was a natural refuge, the obvious centre for a trading population who, building trackways beside the river valley, could barter their tin to vessels coming from both the Atlantic and the Channel sea-routes.

The estuary, alas, is now, and has been through the centuries, silting up. A narrow channel, marked with straggling poles to warn

23

the venturing seamen of the ever-encroaching banks of sand, leads to the once flourishing port. Even the yachtsman dares not hazard the passage that long ago offered shelter and opportunity for trade to Bronze Age seamen.

For the watcher today, crouching amidst the sand-dunes and the tufted grass, looking seaward to where the shallows run, imagination can take a riotous course, picturing line upon line of high-prowed flat-bottomed craft, brightly coloured, their sails abeam, entering the river with the flood tide. What cries and oaths, what turbulence of Mediterranean chatter interspersed with Irish, as the traders ran their vessels on the sand or anchored them to swing midstream; what speedy loading or unloading of cargo between ship and settlement, what feasting, when the work was done, beside a fire of turf and furze; what interchange of vows, with dance and conquest!

The image fades, and the dreamer, stiff from crouching in the dunes, sees how the sand has, through the centuries, invaded the coastal countryside north of Hayle. Hurricanes, in the long-distant past, whipped up the swirling mass into dense clouds which settled on the land below. Whole farmsteads were overwhelmed and now lie buried, while the waste land known as the towans, a mixture of sand and sea-rush – a stiff-stemmed reedy grass planted in old days by the inhabitants to stay the driving sand – stretches through Phillack and Gwithian parishes until the ground rises into the headland of Godrevy Point. Gales and storms have been ever frequent on both north and south Cornish coasts, bringing havoc and disaster with them and a multitude of wrecks, but a hurricane of sand, destroying homes, was the grim fate of these Gwithian farmers near to Hayle. A winter gale will spend its force, the seas grow calm, the rains cease; the sand is a more insidious enemy. During one tempestuous winter of the nineteenth century there was a sudden shifting of the sands, and the long-buried farmstead of Upton was exposed to view, roof and walls preserved like a villa in Pompeii. People came from near and far to gaze in wonder. Then the wind and sand rose in unison, and Upton Barton was buried once again.

Beyond Upton, close to where the river Connor empties its rusty waters into the sea – the river known as the Red because of the residue of tin staining the surface and washing the banks from the old mines near the source – there are other ruins beneath the sand, disturbed from time to time by wandering cattle. Here lies the Oratory of St. Gothian, who gave his name to Gwithian parish and was supposedly a martyr. Today there is nothing left but a few scattered stones, the sand about them seeping red. What manner of man it was who prayed here and preached redemption none can say.

Many a pilgrim, staff in hand, afire with early Christian zeal, set foot in Hayle from Wales and Ireland, to be called, in later years, a Cornish saint. Their names are legion. There are more parishes named after founder-saints scattered across the length and breadth of Cornwall than anywhere in the rest of England. One thing is certain: the saints bore little likeness to latter-day parish priests. Some of them were hermits or holy-men, with a knowledge of herbs and remedies for ills, inheritance of an older lore that could be turned to good account, magic interwoven with the sign of the Cross. They lived on rocks and promontories, beside streams or near to the sea's edge, and the prayers they uttered awoke in the converted a memory of incantations in the past.

Others dwelt closer to their flock, and, like the preaching Methodists of our own times and the worker priests of France at the factory bench, won respect from their fellow-men because of skill with hands as well as with tongue, becoming, without deliberate intent, leaders within a group. As to St. Gothian, whose bones may or may not lie beneath the ruined Oratory on the towans, it is good to think of him streaming for tin somewhere near the Connor source, then descending to the bay to offer thanks, his ankles rusty red and caked with the sand, carrying in his hands as an emblem to faith a thunder-axe or pick.

Other saints, like the Welshman Samson, avoided the likely inhospitality of Hayle and reached Cornwall by way of the Camel estuary. For the approach to Cornwall can be made in many ways, dangerously as of old, like seafarer or saint, braving the short seas and the shifting sands of Hayle and Camel, which can only be recommended to the intrepid with a genius for pilotage; or more leisurely as yachtsman, seeking the broader, safer and more welcoming waters of the Fal and Fowey estuaries, whose seaports, unlike forgotten Hayle, still offer haven to shipping from the world and carry a thriving trade. These estuaries, winding and deeply wooded in their upper reaches, seem a world away from sand-swept Hayle and Camel on the northern coast, though little more than sixteen miles separates Fal from the first and Fowey from the second.

Even the climate is more temperate. Here the rain, no longer driving across high barren ground where the stunted trees are blown backwards by its force, falls in a mizzle. A sluggish indolence pervades. The stranger, coaxing his boat up-river in a sudden windless calm, ignoring the busy harbour, casts anchor with a yawn beside pool or creek, then lolls by the tiller, too idle to row ashore.

A sluggish indolence pervades.

Peace prevails. The tide ebbs. The gently wooded slopes on either side of him that seemed at first sight to touch the water's edge appear more distant. Mud-banks form beneath them, oozing and soft, or little steep-to beaches of grey slate.

Birds, save for the gulls that piloted him to port, have hitherto been absent. Now they are everywhere. Oyster-catchers – sea-pie to the Cornish – with a quick seeping cry, swoop to the mud-banks in a flash of black and white. The smaller redshank and sanderling scurry to probe the slate. Further up-river, where a dead branch from a fallen tree, strung about with seaweed, overhangs the water, a heron stalks, prinking his way like some grave professor fearing to lose a galosh, then suddenly stands and broods, his wings humped, his head buried in his feathers. Later the tide slackens, the trees darken, the birds are hushed, and there is no sound except the whisper of water past the anchor chain until, if the yachtsman is lucky, he will hear, during the magic moments before true dusk falls, the night-jar call. It is a summons unlike any other, churring, low, strangely compelling, so that on first hearing it you must think of neither bird nor beast but of some forgotten species, a scaly lizard cross-bred with a toad. There is no sweetness here, no nightingale passion, no owl foreboding; the call is primitive, insistent, with a rhythmic rise and fall, coming not from the wooded slopes but from open ground beyond, where amidst foxglove and gorse the night-jar crouches.

The silence of the upper reaches of Fowey river, and of those of Fal and Helford too, broken today by the chug of diesel and outboard engine, a passing irritant, was less intense in the distant past, when their forking branches were tidal further inland, and ships of depth could discharge cargoes at the ancient river ports, now sleeping villages by the stream's edge. Gweek and Constantine on Helford, Tregoney on Fal, Lostwithiel on Fowey, knew maritime greatness as late as the sixteenth century, the channels deep enough for vessels to cast anchor or make fast to the stone quays. Another estuary, now sand-barred and impenetrable, cut inland past Tywardreath to St. Blazey bridge, and if the eye follows the course of the marsh between the hills where the railway now runs it becomes instantly perceptible

Tamar bridges.

why King Mark of Cornwall built his fortress on the high ground at Castle Dor, commanding the sea entrances to east and west.

Such, then, was the seafarer's approach to Cornwall in olden times; but the invader from overland had first to ford the Tamar, and the traveller who does this today in his fast-moving car can become, for a brief moment, a Roman legionary or a Saxon king.

There are some thirteen bridges across the Tamar now, the last being only three years old, running parallel to Brunel's railway bridge from Plymouth to Saltash. There were none before the Normans conquered England, and the Romans, like the Saxons, would have forded the river high up-stream, close to the river's source, or pushed on beyond the marshy bed to the high ground above, where some four miles only separate Tamar from the sea. Had ingenious diggers in the past made a vast trench linking the Tamar source with the secondary stream that rises near to it and hurtles down to Marsland Mouth, Cornwall would have been an island. Invasion might, for a decade longer, have been held at bay. As it was the enemy rode and conquered, finding that the high ground formed a backbone across the narrow breadth of Cornwall.

Today a main road covers the same worn track, bearing the traveller to Camelford, where Saxon Egbert defeated the Cornish at Slaughter Bridge. If, unlike Egbert, he has a peaceable nature and a taste for exploration, he may descend from the car, climb the banks and try to find the Tamar's source. It will take him many hours, plodding in frustration from field to field through splashy marsh, until a trickle of water, splurging from a bog and coursing east, makes him shout "Eureka!" to a companion out of earshot three fields away. He may, or may not, have found the Tamar, but whatever the stream may be triumph is complete, and he knows a conqueror's pride.

Chapter Two

IN SEARCH OF ARTHUR AND OF TRISTAN

ARTHUR is to Cornwall what Theseus is to Greece. His myth is everywhere. Here is where Arthur sat or Arthur slept, he feasted upon this stone, he hunted upon these moors; Tintagel was his birthplace, Castle-an-Dinas his hunting-lodge, at Slaughter Bridge by Camelford he received his fatal wound, in the Warbstow Burrows lies his grave. Not in Cornwall only but in Somerset and Wales, and across the Channel to Brittany, Arthur is hero; a Celtic warrior, a Breton prince, a Cornish king. The bards sang his praises, the story-tellers told of his valorous deeds, his battles, his conquests, and the people in after years, when paying tribute to the Saxon kings of England, whispered amongst themselves how Arthur would come again and set them free. Later the chroniclers of mediaeval times wrote how King Arthur introduced the Age of Chivalry, of tilting, jousting, of rescuing maidens beset by magician's wand or marauder's sword, of the search for the Holy Grail; and so the Legend of the Round Table was born.

Myths have their origin in minds seeking consolation, an answer to the conflict between good and evil, but the legend interwoven with the myth, however primitive, is based on an historical fact. There *was* an Arthur, a Christian warrior, perhaps a Cornish chief, who lived at the end of the fifth century A.D. and fought the Saxon kings. The rest is supposition, but the tradition that he was born and lived, fought and died on Cornish soil is so dear to the Cornish heart that, despite the claims of Brittany, Somerset and Wales, it would seem to have foundation in fact, and has come to be part of history. The legend that his magic sword Excalibur was flung by one of his warriors into

His myth is everywhere.

a lake after his death, and his body placed in a barque on the same lake and floated to the vale of Avalon, watched over by three weeping queens, remains a dream in the minds of romantic men.

The story of Arthur is curiously interwoven with that of another Cornish king, who may have been Arthur's contemporary or successor. Mark, or Marcus, was a king of Cornwall during the sixth century or earlier, and his fortress was at Castle Dor, once the stronghold of the chief Gorlois. In the Arthurian legend Gorlois is murdered, and Igraine his wife is seduced by Uther Pendragon and becomes the mother of Arthur. Later, when Arthur is chief or king, his wife Gwinevere is herself seduced by Lancelot, a knight at Arthur's court and well-loved by the king. This theme of seduction

31

and betrayal belongs also to King Mark, who sends his nephew Tristan to bring him an Irish bride, the princess Iseult. The story of the love-potion, given to the pair by Iseult's hand-maiden Bronwyn as the ship carries the bride from Ireland to Cornwall, of their hopeless passion and the jealousy of King Mark, is known the world over, more famous even than Arthur's love for Gwinevere.

Three kings with identical marital troubles . . . this pushes credulity a little far. But since their kingdoms were the same, or perhaps adjoining, the answer would seem to be that one of the kings was the original cuckold and the others misrepresented by later gossiping tongues. The theme of jealous husbands and deceiving lovers has existed since story-telling first began, and in the early centuries A.D. would have been a matter for rib-poking and jest, rather than inspiration for the tales of betrayal, unsought but passionate, described by later poets and writers of prose.

Those who have a bent for place-names and etymology, a fondness for maps old and new, and a desire to poke about in hills and valleys in search of the vanished past, have long found, and will continue to find, pleasure in the chase. Camelot, one of the legendary seats of Arthur's court, and the small town of Camelford were synonymous to enthusiasts of other days, not only because of the latter's proximity to Slaughter Bridge, where as an historical fact the Cornish fought and were defeated by the Saxons, but also because it is within five miles or so of the ruined castle of Tintagel – which, awkwardly for the same enthusiasts, turned out to have been built in Norman times. Cadbury Hill in Somerset, where archaeologists are digging now, may yet turn out to be the Camelot of legend, but while we await their findings Cornish claims for other Arthurian sites are strong.

Charles Henderson, perhaps Cornwall's finest scholar, with a genius for research, who died in 1933 at the early age of thirty-three, quoted the Welsh Triads as saying that "Kelly-wick in Cornwall" was the favourite residence of King Arthur; thus Kellywick or Killibury, a hill castle set high between the Allen and the Camel rivers, was, in his opinion, the obvious site. Kelly, in Cornish, means a grove of trees; today the place consists of two circular earthen ditches splayed

The ruined castle of Tintagel built in Norman times.

about with thorn and bramble; but with such a setting, and commanding views of the Camel estuary and an enemy approaching from the west, the vast enclosed circle must, some fifteen hundred years ago, have been a fortress of great strength.

Those of us who were brought up on Tennyson's *Idylls of the King* and Malory's *Morte d'Arthur* have to put aside memories of the turreted castles and armoured knights which illustrated our childish versions. The hill-castles of the first centuries A.D. were defensive circular earthworks, sometimes three trenches deep, and within these ramparts were wooden huts where the occupants ate and slept. The finest hill-castle in all Cornwall is Castle-an-Dinas, above St.

Columb, west of the great highway that runs across Cornwall's backbone. Here the inner circle is about 1700 feet by 1500, with space for stabling, granaries, bakehouses, dining-chambers, sleeping-quarters and a whole army of warriors. Whatever kings ruled Cornwall before the Norman Conquest, Castle-an-Dinas would have been their strongest base, 700 feet high, commanding road and sea. The other hill-castles are more in the nature of outposts, watch-towers or the fortresses of minor rulers.

Another place-name that figures largely in Arthurian legend was the place of Carlyon, where the King held Court with Gwinevere. Carlyon – Caerlydan in A.D. 969 – is a smaller earthwork or round south of the river Fal, and particularly interesting for the fact that about a mile-and-a-half distant is Nansavallan or Avallen, Cornish for apple tree.

Avallen, Avalon, where the weeping queens bore Arthur? Excitement grows. A stream runs close to Nansavallan, entering one of the long reaches of the Fal. In centuries long past this would have been wider, deeper. Did Arthur, wounded in battle, perhaps at Slaughter Bridge as tradition holds, travel by litter to his southern fortress at Carlyon and, dying, ask his faithful followers to place him in a boat upon the river near to Avallen, where the apple orchards grew?

Roads, farms, bungalows, must be forgotten, the changing contours of intervening years blotted from sight. This trek across hill and stream and valley, however frustrating, fires the amateur sleuth. The answer is buried in time, the search is all.

There is no fever like the quest for the past, as warming to the blood as a dig for hidden treasure, and those who participate are lost to present ills. I had an uncle once, my mother's brother, who was a fanatic in the cause. He vowed that all of Shakespeare's manuscripts, written by Bacon, lay buried fathoms deep in the bed of the river Wye. How far he waded, how long he probed, I do not know, but he died aged eighty-odd, his thesis still unproven. Perhaps the infection is inherited; all I know is that I have scoured many a muddied ditch and brambled hedge believing myself to be treading first in Arthur's, then in Tristan's, footsteps. My husband, with a soldier's professional eye and an appreciation of high ground, declared that Castle-an-Dinas and Castle Dor could have been held in old days against all comers. Tintagel, as a landing place for Tristan with his uncle's bride Iseult, he laughed to scorn. Not even a goat in charge of a flat-bottomed punt would beach his craft there. Hayle, perhaps, since Iseult came from Ireland, or even Camel, but the Fal more likely than either if Carlyon was to be the greeting-place, or, if Mark preferred to welcome his bride at Castle Dor, then the Par or Fowey estuaries.

How often we have climbed with field-glasses and maps, elated and discouraged in turn, spurred on by the insistence of Sir Arthur Quiller-Couch, who had it from a Professor Loth, who had transcribed it from the earliest extant manuscript of the Tristan series – *Le Roman de Tristan*, by the twelfth-century chronicler Béroul – that King Mark's palace was at Lancien, the ancient rendering of Lantyan, now a farmstead close to the Fowey river by Castle Dor. Excavations in 1936 and 1937 on the site of Castle Dor, suggested by Dr. Singer

He hunted upon these moors.

and undertaken by C. A. Ralegh Radford and the Cornwall Excavation Committee, proved the scholars right. They dated the first hill-fort at Castle Dor as early as the second century B.C., when it was a fortified village, the findings suggesting that the inhabitants traded in tin and had Breton connections.

During the Roman occupation of Cornwall, lasting more than three centuries, the site fell into disuse. Later, about the fifth century A.D., the centre of the fortress was adapted as a chieftain's dwelling-place, with one large hall for the ruler and porters' lodges by the entry gates. Here, beyond all doubt, was the original Lancien, fortress-palace of King Mark, husband of Iseult. A year later, in 1939, came World War Two. The digging stopped, never to be resumed.

Today, in 1966, Castle Dor bears no trace of excavation but has reverted once again to tumbling earth and brambled ditch. This spring the centre of the site, where Mark's Great Hall once stood, some 90 feet long, aisled, with timbered roof and gabled porch, was under plough. All is buried now; stables, granaries, porters' lodges, chieftain's hall lie confused and intermingled with the huts of the Iron Age settlers, never to be disturbed again by pick and spade. Money is not forthcoming, or interest deep enough, to support another venture. The dream of seeing the whole site – the first foundations of the Breton traders – laid bare, the restoration of Mark's palace to near original form, remains a dream.

The wanderer, with the old legends vivid in his memory, can still stand upon the outer bank at Castle Dor, looking first westward to the sea where the Par estuary once cut into the coast, then eastward to the Fowey river, winding beneath St. Sampson's church at Golant to the wooded slopes below Lantyan farm. It was at a chapel of St. Sampson, according to the French chronicler Béroul, that Queen Iseult heard Mass; it was beside the river that she trysted with her lover while the jealous king hovered in an orchard close at hand. Place-names upon an old map of Lantyan farm are significant – Mark's Gate, Pilfer (postern?) Gate and Prior's Meadow. It is possible that on the site where the farmhouse now stands, or nearer to the river, the King had a separate dwelling-place, with the Queen's

Today Castle Dor bears no trace of excavation.

quarters beside it, giving more shelter and greater privacy than did the soldiers' garrison on the hill at Castle Dor. A stream rises beneath the fortress and descends through sloping fields to Woodget Pyll, and so to Fowey river. It is now only a trickle of water beside the lane or track, but less than a century ago the old people in the neighbourhood called the stream Deraine Lake, saying that in days gone by it formed a lake, with swans upon it, and that a King had made it for his Queen. Deraine Lake . . . Lac de la Reine? This is a strange tradition to come down through fifteen hundred years and be remembered still.

There are swans in Woodget Pyll today, and at high water, when the incoming tide seeps over the mud-banks and the creek becomes a lake indeed, you can see them breast the flood, leaving a path behind like a vessel's wake. The stroll beside Woodget Pyll and up to the lane above, beside the woods, past Lantyan farm and down to the further creek beneath the viaduct, became a favourite walk of ours in latter days, the search for Tristan constantly in mind. Islands, formed by the mud-flats in each creek when the tide withdrew, could have been the fighting ground where Tristan challenged Morholt the Irish messenger to single combat, as the chronicles relate, leaving him to swim to safety – a cut-and-thrust affair on foot with both contenders floundering in mud.

The farcical nature of the struggle makes sense with earlier traditions, for Béroul, unhampered by images of knightly courtesy, describes the exploits of his hero Tristan with a lively gusto. Mark, Iseult, Tristan form a triangle of jealous husband, faithless wife and ardent lover, the two young people bent on deceit. Scenes are clown-like in their simplicity, designed to make the listeners split their sides with laughter. King Mark, thinking to trap his wife in bed, sprinkles flour upon the floor beside it, so as to catch the imprint of Tristan's naked feet, but the wily lover, smiling at the other's frustration, leaps into the connubial couch from sprinting distance, leaving the flour untouched. Hence, no doubt, the famous "saut Tristan," the later prowess of the courteous knight. Béroul, again, tells how Tristan, disguised as a pilgrim, waited by the ford called Mal Pas, in expectation of the Queen passing over it to Carlyon. This was no chivalrous gesture, but a plot between them so that she might bestride his shoulders, and when he tripped and they tumbled in the mud together, taking some while to disentangle, the Queen could afterwards swear to her lord the King that she had lain with no man save a pilgrim. My husband, to whom I told this version, was disconcerted, saying I had spoilt a boyhood image.

We drove once more to the banks of the river Fal and stood at Malpas, the Mal Pas of the poem, looking down upon the intersection of the waters between the Tresillian and the Truro reaches, where the passenger ferry crosses still. The tide was high, the rivers wide, small sailing-craft rocked at their moorings, and the mud-flats

Malpas.

where Tristan and the Queen had tumbled were well and truly covered. My husband, searching the scene with his field-glasses, was overcome with a sudden nostalgia due to more personal causes, reminding me that here at anchor in his motor-boat *Ygdrasil* we had spent a night of honeymoon, and somewhere beneath the mud lay, not the traces of Tristan and Iseult, but a beloved little dish-mop that had been on board since he first launched his boat, and which he had missed, and sighed for, during five-and-twenty years. I needed no reminding.

We pushed on, ignoring the residential St. Clement above us, once the forest of Moresk – where, Béroul said, Tristan and Iseult had escaped from Mark and hidden during weeks – and after passing through Truro looked once more for the buried palace of Carlyon and the apple-orchards of Avalon. Woods and streams abounded, cars hummed by us on the road, but the apple trees remained elusive. "Perhaps," I said, "none of it is true, and there never was a boat, nor a dying Arthur, at least not here"; but he clung stoutly to his dream of weeping queens, and we struggled through woods to the muddied creek that runs into the Fal, and pictured a low barque with pointed prow moving down-river on an ebbing tide to enter the estuary and the sea beyond.

"What then?" I asked.

"The Lost Land of Lyonesse and the Islands of the Blest," answered my husband, lowering his field-glasses, his vision of the past undimmed, his faith in the future steadfast.

Whether Arthur died at sea or in the apple-orchards of Nansavallan, the fate of Tristan seems more certain, though Béroul broke off in the midst of inspiration, leaving his poem unfinished, to be added to by others. Later versions tell how Tristan escaped to Brittany, and finding another Iseult was faithless to the first. Wounded by a poisoned weapon he sends for his earlier love to come and heal him, with the request that the ship bearing her shall carry a white sail, or, if she loves him no longer, that she shall bid the seamen hoist it black. He waits, mortally wounded, for the vessel to arrive, but the second Iseult, jealous, watching the horizon, tells him that a ship with black sails is approaching and, despairing, Tristan dies. The Cornish Queen, faithful to the last, lands on Breton soil, and finding her lover dead dies too.

This version, with its strange echo of an older, different, legend and the return of Theseus, after destroying the Minotaur in Crete, to Athens where his father Aegeus waited, the signal of the son's safety to be the hoisting of a white sail, but black if his son had died, can be discounted. Tristan died in Cornwall, whether by a poisoned spear from the hand of his rival, King Mark, or a wound received in battle, none can prove. More probably the latter. For no more than a mile and a half from King Mark's fortress at Castle Dor, the old Lancien, there stands a pillar, some seven feet high, and carved upon it the

There stands a pillar some seven feet high.

inscription "Drustans Hic Iacit/Cvnomori Filius." Commorus, or Quonomorius, has been identified by scholars as Marcus, or Mark, King of Cornwall, and Drustans as Tristan, so for those of us less lettered who look upon it the inscription translates "Tristan Lies here, Son of Mark."

The stone did not always stand by the Four Turnings but lay somewhere near by, the exact position unrecorded. Perhaps if the fields on either side of the old crossroads had been dug, like the site at Castle Dor, the burial grounds of warriors would have been discovered and the tomb of Tristan found. The inscription Son of Mark upon the stone suggests that even if the love story were true, even closer and

The last outpost of an aged Cornish king.

more illicit than the chroniclers told, the King, when his son died, did not feel himself dishonoured. The pillar, a memorial to a fighting prince, has withstood time and speculation since the fifth century A.D.

No stone commemorating the King has ever shown itself, revealed in the turned earth by spade or plough, but another mile and a half seaward, overlooking the great sweep of Par Bay, there stands an old house built upon fourteenth-century foundations. It is named Kilmarth. The word, in Cornish, means Retreat of Mark. It is strange and moving to believe that this spot, once the home of Professor Singer – who was the first to suggest that Castle Dor should be excavated – was the last outpost of an aged Cornish king who, with passion spent and jealousy forgotten, looked out in peace across the open sea.

Chapter Three

CLIMATE

SOME hundred and fifty million years ago, so we are told, Cornwall, or what existed of it, was washed by tropical seas, and then when the Ice Age came it was gripped by freezing winds. Through the long centuries that followed the climate changed again, to warmer summers and wet winters, until in historical times – as today – there was little variation between the two and the peninsula bathed in a kind of perpetual spring. Not the spring of brilliant sunshine and cloudless skies envisaged on the travel posters, but a more temperate affair, as if a mild February had prolonged itself into a damp June, a mellow mistiness pervading, and the visitor, swimming trunks and sun-tan lotion in his bathing bag, is puzzled to find that although he can both smell and hear the sea he cannot see it. The white mist, drifting inland from the coast, dissolves in patches, and for no reason a sequestered valley will be free, or a village tucked away in the fold of some forbidding hill, and the two will be wrapped for half the day in a near-tropical stillness, while the coasts and the headlands shiver.

This difference in temperature, this vagary of weather, varies from mile to mile with a kind of lunatic perversity. Here, by the Fowey estuary, the rain will fall steadily from dawn till dusk, yet across country on the Camel never a cloud be seen; but more irritating still, for those of us who clump about in oilskins and sea-boots on a midsummer day, is the telephone call from London telling us that the rest of England swelters in a heatwave of equatorial intensity.

Primroses found on a morning in January, daffodils blooming before St. Valentine's Day, camellias and rhododendron coming into bud and bloom in early February are consolation but not altogether

44

Cornwall will take a shower every day in the week, and two on Sundays.

compensation for the summer basking we too often miss. Anticyclones pass us by. Depressions seek us out. The prevailing wind of Cornwall, sou'westerly, damp and in essence mild, is the cause of all our grumbles, but without it Cornwall would lose its character and become a barren and bitter land.

A writer in the first part of the seventeenth century put the matter very plainly. "The air being cleansed with frequent Winds and the Tides, is very pure and healthful, so that the Inhabitants are rarely troubled with any infectious Diseases; yet being sharp and piercing, such as have been sick, especially Strangers, recover but slowly. The Seasons of the Year are something different from those in other Parts; the Spring is more backward, the Summer more temperate, Autumnal Fruits later, their Harvest rarely being ripe enough for the Barn till near Michaelmas, but then well digested, and the Winter, by reason of the warm Breezes, much milder, for they have Frost and Snow but very seldom and then they soon vanish. Nevertheless, the Country being surrounded by the Sea, is subject to such violent Storms, that not only uncover their Houses, but rend up their Hedges, and hinder the Growth of their Trees. One kind of them, which they count most furious, they call a Flaw or Flagh."

I have not come across the flaw or flagh, although the *Glossary of West Cornwall* mentions flaad, i.e., "puffed out with flatulency, as cattle after too much green food." The word makes sense. I have known many a flatulent wind in sailing days now past when puffs of sudden violence swept down across Lantic Bay, causing the boat to heel over, scuppers awash. The fury was only temporary and soon passed, and the boat was on an even keel once more; however, like indigestion, the impression lingered, Nature's warning to keep a steadier hand upon the tiller before the next belch blew.

A Londoner called Walter White, who walked to Land's End during the July of 1854, found that the Cornish summer "produced on some constitutions a feeling of languor and depression unknown in a drier atmosphere. These are considerations not to be lost sight of in discussing the important questions of change of air. Whether on the cliffs of Devonshire or Cornwall, there were few days on which one

46

Here, by the Fowey estuary, the rain will fall steadily from dawn till dusk.

did not find an overcoat acceptable, and the evenings were almost invariably chilly." He also repeated the popular saying that Cornwall will take a shower every day in the week and two on Sundays. As Mr. White continued his walk further west he observed that "at times a gusty drizzle sets in and lasts for two or three weeks, making everything miserable out of doors, and damp within."

The comfort of his nightly lodgings brought satisfaction, for he seldom paid more than one and sixpence for two meals and his bed. The weather, however, obsessed him, and he noted that the terrific winds "carried the salt spray ten miles inland, so that it may be tasted on window-panes, and the blades of corn. At times it destroys whole acres of wheat in the fields near the sea. You will see some of the old manor houses built facing the east or the south-east, regardless of the view from the front windows; the builders having preferred a site where the rear of the house would be sheltered by a low hill and a belt of trees."

Yet when the few days of delight appear, to be remembered ever after with thanksgiving, they dawn with what a shimmering haze and almost Grecian beauty, the sea milky white in Par Bay because of the streams that flow into it from the clay-hills beyond Luxulyan. No sound but the lap of water past the bows as the boat, like a phantom ship, floats across the bay to Black Head, there to lie at anchor between Gwendra Point and Ropehaven. Vessels in old days used this as anchorage, sheltering from the south-west winds, and at low spring tides, stumbling about amongst the shingle and the weeds, you may find traces of the jetty that stood there once, the flat stones gleaming dark and grey beneath the water's surface. Swimming is cold, for the beach shelves swiftly to several fathoms, and the sea has a saltier taste than nearer home at Pridmouth. The beaches accessible by road are black with people, heads bob about in the water a mile distant, and little chugging craft or swift canoes weave in and out amongst them like minnows.

Here, in the old Ropehaven, all is peace, the long afternoon drifts by, until a slow ripple against the anchor chain makes the boat swing to a leisurely dance and the helmsman becomes restive, sensing the first whisper of a breeze. The lazy wallow beneath the sun is over. Sails are hoisted, the anchor raised, sheets made fast, and we are homeward bound across the bay, a beam wind from the north-west whipping us back to Fowey. We throw mackerel lines astern and make them fast, and while one of us is intent on the trimming of sails the other stares towards the land, the clay-hills hard and white on the western skyline. Then the slope of the Gribbin peninsula approaches, bracken-covered, green, and beyond it, hull-down between its coverage of trees, two chimney-tops and the grey roof of Menabilly.

Coming to the harbour entrance we wind in the lines.

Coming to the harbour entrance we wind in the lines, and on one of them find a limp and long-dead fish whose protesting struggles neither of us felt. The breeze dies, the tide is slack, and with infinite cunning born of long experience the helmsman brings the sailing craft to her moorings at the opening of Pont Pyll. The buoy is lifted, the sails lowered and stowed, the fish cleaned, and as the stringy guts are thrown into the air all of Fowey's gulls appear, wheeling, screaming, until one more voracious than its fellows dives to the patch of water where the mess has fallen and gulps it wholesale.

This is the moment for pausing, for lighting a cigarette and glancing around to appraise the visiting craft, anchored in the pool below Polruan. Fowey town has been in shadow since early afternoon, but Polruan, and all the eastern hills sloping to Pont Creek, are caught by the vanishing sun, with the ripple on the water dusky red. It is a moment of satisfaction and tranquillity. Although we have been away only six hours or so, and covered no more than twice that amount in miles out and back, it is the repose of journey's end. Tomorrow, and tomorrow, and tomorrow . . . But when tomorrow dawns it is to find that the promise of repetition is not fulfilled. The wind has backed to the sou'west during the night, the sky is overcast, and even as we rub our eyes and stare out across the grass the first rain comes, softly at first, nothing much, a pittering irritation, but gradually increasing to the slanting, steady fall that means a day indoors, the paying of bills and writing of letters, and a self-imposed twenty-minute shuffle after tea under the shrouded gloom of dripping trees.

Thus the Cornish climate, accepted by the natives with a philosophical shrug of the shoulders, endured by later settlers with less fortitude, and braved by the summer visitor, who, with expectations whipped by posters depicting bikini-clad lollers on golden sands, tells himself that if yesterday was wet tomorrow will be fine.

The traveller from London, Mr. Walter White, was fortunate in that when he finally achieved Land's End the day was calm. A Frenchman, Monsieur Alphonse Esquiros, who followed in his wake some ten years later, just over a century ago, was not so lucky. He was greeted first by a dense black fog, and then by a storm. Taking refuge in a school near Sennen Cove, he was invited to sit down on a bench amongst the pupils, while the teacher complained to him with bitterness that the district was either too hot or too cold, and at all times uninhabitable. When the wind blows, he was assured, a man wants two other men to hold his hair on his head. After this he was not surprised to find, on the faces of the inhabitants of Sennen, what he expressed as "a sort of melancholy gravity, the women, especially, with a stern, sad air, features hard as a rock, and foreheads prematurely wrinkled." Tales of a whole family perishing together in a squall depressed him still further, and he was glad to

"The Blue Ship" painted by Cornish fisherman Alfred Wallis.

return to his lodging in Penzance. Although impressed by the stoicism of the Cornish people, and their apparent inurement to poverty and hardship, he sought in vain, so he told his readers, even on a Sunday, for the scenes of domestic joy and happiness so sweetly described by English poets. The peasants, he found, spoke little, and it was difficult to discover the reason for this silence, which at times resembled coldness. Was it indifference to their mode of life? Was it resignation, or that species of tacit contentment which the conscious-ness of a strict duty accomplished imparted to a man?

The reserve which he observed in the Cornish character was something sturdier, more deep-rooted, a self-sufficiency bred in the bone through centuries of independence and being largely his own master, with a natural scepticism and suspicion of the stranger who asked questions. Even the stories they told the Frenchman, of fear-some gales and mass drownings, recounted with grave faces, would have been part of the dramatic genius which all inherit, for despite innate reserve the Cornish, like the Irish, are great raconteurs. Or were. Today the art is dying, and the need for self-expression with it. No longer during winter evenings are the shutters closed, the lamps lighted, and the family gathered round the hearth to listen to old tales, as they did, to my own memory, thirty-five years ago. Tele-vision has us enslaved and entertained, and we cannot so much as hear the wind outside. So, although the captive Cornish viewer broadens his general knowledge, he loses his priceless heritage of being different: taste, amusement, opinion, outlook become uniform.

It is only when a greater gust of wind than usual heralds a sou'westerly gale, and trees and electricity cables crash together, that Cornishmen "One and All" find themselves in isolation once again. Stoves are extinguished, screens are silent, and those who are lucky enough to have a box of candles at the back of a kitchen drawer grope their way to bed. Outside they can hear the full fury of the storm, the lashing rain, the roar of the distant sea, as Cornwall's climate, caring not a jot for time or century, behaves as it always has done, always will do, tearing the hills and valleys without pity throughout the night, to spend itself, at dawn, in a sullen calm.

Chapter Four

THE CORNISH HUNDREDS AND MADRON WELL

CORNWALL was originally divided into sections known as "Hundreds," though it is not certain quite how and why they came into being. Charles Henderson did not believe that they grew casually from the separation of Celtic tribes, but thought that they were created at a particular time, with the intention of dividing Cornwall into districts in accordance with its geographical features.

The lists go back to the eleventh century, but the Hundreds must have been in existence long before. Their names have a fascinating ring, like all things Cornish: Penwith, Kerrier, Pyder, Powder, Trigg, East Wivel, West Wivel, Lesnowth, Stratton.

The old maps show the nine divisions very clearly, and with the aid of a Cornish glossary it is even possible to hazard a guess at the derivation of these names. It seems as if Stratton, meaning highway, was the first Hundred, for near Stratton town itself was the original highway from the Tamar. The Stratton Hundred starts by the Devon border at Marsland Mouth on the north coast, merging into the second Hundred, Lesnowth, a few miles north of Dizzard Head. Lesnowth, meaning "the new width", and Stratton Hundreds possess some of the finest coast-line in all Cornwall, especially Stratton, where the high coombes or valleys plunge steeply to the sea and buildings, mercifully, are few. Tintagel is in Lesnowth, and Boscastle, and the wildest moors east of Camelford. The Hundred of Lesnowth turns to Trigg, which derives from third and thus means the Third Hundred. It follows the north coast down as far as the Camel estuary, stretching inland beyond Bodmin and the old highway south to

Lostwithiel. From the Camel estuary to St. Agnes Head the Hundred of Pyder takes over (Pyder meaning fourth), its eastern border still the great ridge or backbone of Cornwall dividing the north coast from the south.

Beyond St. Agnes Head the stretch of land comprising the towans, the Hayle estuary and the whole of the Land's End peninsula, including Mount's Bay on the south coast, forms the Hundred of Penwith. There are three renderings of Penwith – "the last promon-

The Stratton Hundred starts by the Devon border at Marsland Mouth.

tory,'' ''promontory on the left'' and, more intriguing still, ''the headland of slaughter.'' High on these moors of West Penwith are the
many quoits and tombs that were the burial places of those first
settlers in prehistoric times. Whether they died in fighting sea-borne
invaders, or in the tribal battle amongst themselves, nobody can tell,
but ''the headland of slaughter'' points to an ancient tradition that in
those days of long ago Penwith was a place of strife.

Kerrier, meaning ''high coast or border,'' runs from Port Levan on
Mount's Bay to Lizard Point, and thence to the west bank of the Fal.
East of the Fal Powder, the seventh Hundred and the ''place of
oaks,'' runs from St. Mawes to Fowey haven. It is well named. This is
the most wooded part of the whole Cornish peninsula, and, with its
rivers Fal and Fowey, the most fertile. Powder gives way to West and
East Wivel, the first running from the Fowey estuary to Looe river,
the second to where the Tamar estuary enters Plymouth Sound.
Wivel, or Wyvell's, means the ''shire of Welshmen or strangers,'' and
this most eastern district of Cornwall could well have been, in early
days, given over to intruders, who crossed from the Welsh borders
into Devon, and so to Stratton highway in the north.

The nine Hundreds, following the entire coast-line of Cornwall,
now make sense: the Highway, the New Width, the Third and
Fourth Hundreds, the Left Promontory or Headland of Slaughter,
the High Coast, the Place of Oaks, the West and East Hundreds of
Strangers or Welshmen.

These Hundreds, through succeeding centuries, made convenient
units for the administration of the law, for tithing and parochial
systems, and for the manorial rights of the feudal lords; but for those
of us more interested in persons than in systems, in customs than in
jurisdiction, it is stimulating to discover that, the further west we
travel in Cornwall, the further back we go to earlier days and earlier
ways, to a greater degree of saw and superstition, even to a change in
accent and intonation. The Cornish in the East speak with a burr like
the men of Devon – or did, a generation ago, before the advent of
television; and this is understandable when it is remembered that
they live in West and East Wivel, the shire of Strangers. There is little

variation as one passes to mid-Cornwall, to the Third and Fourth Hundreds and the Place of Oaks, but come to Kerrier, the "High Coast," and above all to Penwith, west of the river Hayle, and a singsong cadence of another pitch falls upon the ear; even the vocabulary is, or was, quite different. It was at Mousehole, the little fishing-port on Mount's Bay in West Penwith, that the last inhabitant to speak the old Cornish language died in 1777; it was to Madron Well, in the same Hundred, that women brought their infants in May month to be cured of shingles, wild-fires, tetters and other diseases, and to be fortified against witchcraft and the evil eye.

Today the claw of Cornwall comprising West Penwith and Kerrier, from Clodgy Point on the Atlantic to Lizard Point on the English Channel, attracts more tourist traffic than perhaps anywhere else in Cornwall. Coaches, cars, caravans spawn by the wayside, park on the headlands, blacken the coves and inlets during summer months from Whitsun to September; but come the equinox on the twenty-third of the month, coinciding with the end of school holidays, and they vanish overnight, leaving the claw to its former barren splendour.

Some five-and-thirty years ago you could still ride or drive in pony and jingle about the roads and byways of "the headland of slaughter," even in the summer, and be the one intruder. A friend and I once pitched a small tent between Cape Cornwall and Botallack Head, on an evening of great calm. I can remember now the stillness of sea and sky, the remote wash of the Atlantic against the rocks below, our only companions gulls and ravens. We cooked bacon over a furze fire, and the satisfying smell of it, with the bitter-hot tang of the white ashes, is in my nostrils now. The night came slowly, and we lay with the flap of the tent open, to watch the stars. Then, if never before or since, it seemed possible to become one with those sleepers, long dead, whose bones were ashes like the ashes of our fire, scattered beneath the tombs of West Penwith. They, as we did, must have cooked food over a furze fire, and lain awake and watched the stars. They, unlike us, would have stood sentinel upon the cliffs, awaiting, perhaps, with excitement and fear the thrusting prows of invading craft, line upon line of them, low and narrow, surging inward from the sea. Waking at dawn, the flap of the tent still open, I saw framed on the far horizon, quite motionless, the sea a glassy calm, a full-rigged ship. Whither bound, where from, we never discovered. The sight was a rare one even in those days, but the glimpse of it made perfect a moment of great beauty, never to stale with time or vanish from memory.

Later that day the weather broke, and we sought refuge from a thunderstorm at the Land's End, in a shed with a tin roof that shook and rattled as if in the power of demons. My companion, fearful of thunder since a child, clasped her hands over her ears and moaned. The pony, unleashed from the shafts of the jingle, trembled beside us. Only a few hours had passed since the still dawn, and I thought how, had we stayed in our eyrie near Cape Cornwall, the storm would have come upon us unawares, tearing the tent in two like a pocket-handkerchief, dragging us with it, and the grazing pony, terror-struck, have broken perhaps from his tethering-rope to gallop inland, or, worse, plunged headlong to the sea. Small wonder that the inhabitants of West Penwith were superstitious, fearful, seeking to protect themselves and their children against the elements, the evil eye and things unknown.

The west Cornish term for nightmare was to be "hilla-ridden" or to "have the stag." The first meant that a man passed his time in an agony of tormenting dreams, the second that he had a feeling of weight upon his chest, preventing breathing. A cure for these, as well as a preventive of lesser, physical ills, was to "crame" – to crawl on all fours – through the ringed stone of the Mên-an-Tol, or better still to wash in the waters of Madron Well. This spring in early March my son and I set forth in search of the healing waters of the well. Neither of us suffered from tetters or even cramp, but I had read of the poor cripple John Trelilie, who for all his life had been forced to walk upon his hands, until in 1650 a cure was wrought on him. Three times in a dream he was told to wash himself in Madron Well, and crawling there he did so, and ever after walked upon his feet.

The well is difficult to find. Although marked on the map, a mile or so above Madron church, the sign to it in March was drooping, rusted, pointing to the ground. We tried three fields in turn and found no water, then seeing a farmhouse on a distant hill we decided to enquire, a method of exploration I despise. A young woman came along the farm-track towards us, busward bound, perhaps, for she tittuped on high heels and swung a shopping bag. We asked for Madron Well, and smiling she pointed to our right, to a deep thicket set in a valley between sloping fields, marred by electric pylons.

"It's somewhere there," she said, "or so my husband says. He wanted to take me once, but the ground is dirty. I've lived at the farm eight years and never seen it yet."

She waved her hand and prinked her way towards the road, while heedless of briar and bramble we plunged into the thicket. The way was tortuous and damp, the once trodden path oozing mud and overgrown with tangled bushes. The thicket branches, closely inter-twined, impeded progress, and long bramble stems clung to our shoulders and wound themselves about our chests, giving us in very truth "the stags." Somewhere close by, yet out of reach, must be the well, and to this place John Trelilie must have crawled, and all those women through the centuries to plunge their children naked.

We found it at last, hard by the ugly pylon, in a clearing within stone walls. The water was dank and still. I was not satisfied. This must be the baptistry, spoken of in later books, where Christian mothers with unconscious pagan leanings brought infants to be baptised. I sought the magic healing spring itself, which should rise from the ground clear and never stagnant, bubbling out of unknown depths beneath the soil. A trickle of water underneath a stone a few yards distant, and in the profoundest tangle of the thicket, made me rejoice. My son, more sceptical, declared it was a drain. Nevertheless the bubbles rose, and breaking off a twig I turned it nine times against the sun; and though my son was no longer a child to strip, and then be rolled in something warm and laid to sleep above the spring, with a piece of his clothing hung by on a thorn to act as votive offering, I told him the spirits were appeased, and both of us were cleansed. A piece of tissue was all I could find to splay upon the thorn, and as I turned and left it, hanging there above the spring, I thought of poor John Trelilie washing his wasted limbs.

The water within the well was dank and still.

We hacked our way back through the thicket and up the valley, and when we came to the rutted lane where the car was waiting we saw an old man standing there, leaning upon a stick. He needed no telling; he knew where we had been. "They never go there now," he said, "'tis all forgotten. The people hereabouts are strangers." He jerked his head towards a row of council houses on the road three fields away. "Mostly from Birmingham," he added. I wondered about the young woman from the farmhouse who had not wanted to dirty her shoes. We paused, waiting for more. He stared down to the valley and the hidden spring, then sighed and shook his head. "The Cornish have all gone," he said, "they've all gone down the line." He wished us good-day and ambled off, still shaking his head and sighing.

As we climbed into the car and drove away we murmured to each other the lilting phrase, "They've all gone down the line." It made us think of farmsteads and cottages bereft, of Cornish emigrants with packs upon their backs, of stern-faced fathers and wan-eyed mothers and small crying children, setting forth from Penzance station to some unknown destination beyond the Tamar, leaving their homes to aliens from the Midlands, eager to offer bed-and-breakfast to the wayfarer, and, when winter came, to seek amusement in the bingo-halls of Camborne and Redruth.

Once, if not in the old man's time at least in the memory of his grandfather and great-grandfather, there was wilder entertainment in West Penwith. Those who were not "hilla-ridden" or suffering from the "stag" would ride away from Madron to parishes further afield, to Sancreed or to Zennor on the coast, there to waylay married couples on their wedding-night and flog them to bed with cords and sheep-spans, in the belief that such treatment would bring them happiness and ensure increase in stock. Many a bridal chamber was invaded for this purpose, the wedding guests armed with stones concealed in a stocking, and the first one of the happy couple hit would point to the sex of their first-born.

No rough hilarity for those who went down the line, no cracking of whips, no turbulent song, no plunging of stark babies into wells, no "craming" through the stones. A soberer life awaited them, in work-shops or at the factory bench, and the gas-lamps of the cities would not have the lure of a lanthorn's light. Their children, baptised decently in church or chapel, would never know the ice-cold shock of water from a spring, or the sudden warmth of the sun upon naked limbs.

Down the line, we murmured, down the line . . . and as we descended from Madron to Penzance a sudden mist enfolded us, blanketing behind us the whole of West Penwith. The high land was obscured, with the sweep of the curving bay, for the mist, rolling in-land from the sea and clammy cold, shut out the present with the past and all was lost. The coming of the mist was sad, symbolic of a vanishing age, as though the last headland and the promontory of slaughter were in themselves taboo, and closed to strangers.

It was too late that day for further exploration, but we were resolved, before the week ended, to return. Cornwall's fifth Hundred held other secrets still.

Chapter Five

THE LEGEND OF PENROSE

"WHAT remains of the old mansion of Penrose, in Sennen, stands on a low and lonely site at the head of a narrow valley through which a mill-brook winds, with many abrupt turns, for about three miles, thence to Penberth Cove." These words, from the old book of *Hearthside Stories*, had imprinted themselves in my mind, for a modern map says nothing of lonely sites or winding brooks, and the red circle I had drawn about the name Penrose might cover, for all I knew, a caravan camp dumped above a stream.

Here is the trouble when searching for the past. Imagination conjures up bare hills and wilder shores, manors with tall chimneys flanked by courtyards, only to find, when catching up with the present, that rows of houses or perhaps a filling-station dominate the hill, that a smuggler's cove has beach-tents and the foundations of a Tudor home are hidden beneath a stuccoed Victorian villa or modern bungalow.

"We can only drive there and find out," my son said firmly, "and if there's nothing left . . ." He shrugged in resignation and we set forth once again, with maps and field-glasses, to that "promontory of slaughter," West Penwith. As we drove, some fifty miles or more, I told him the story in the same language as I remembered it, as it was no doubt told in countless cottages on winter nights before an open hearth in bygone days, with the rain beating upon the window-panes outside.

"Long, long ago," I said, "some three hundred years or maybe more, there was an ancient family called Penrose, living in the manor house that bore their name, in Sennen parish. The country there-abouts was wild and naked, exposed to the salt wind from the sea, and in winter the rain fretted the wheat out of the ground, so that it was washed away and useless, the only land for cultivation being the close places between the hills. The head of the family in those days was Ralph Penrose, who as a young man had led a seafaring life, and when he succeeded to his father's estate so great still was his love for sailing and the sea that he built himself a ship and became what they called then a fair-trader, or, as we say today, a smuggler. He was never a pirate, as some of them were, or robbed the poor, but would sail across to France with his devoted crew, most of them poor relations who could find no better means of living, and then bring back merchandise to Sennen, and distribute it amongst the people in the neighbourhood and the members of his own household. He traded for the love of the game, as did his cousin William, as great an adventurer as himself.

"Sorrow came to Ralph one autumn, when his wife died of a fever, and from then onwards he seemed to take a dislike to the land, being at sea more than ever and taking his only son with him, a lad of seven. He would do this even in winter, leaving his estate to be managed by his younger brother John. One winter's night, before the turn of the year, Ralph Penrose was sailing home from France with his ship well laden, his crew in good heart and his cousin William and his young son aboard, when a gale sprang up some miles south of the Land's End, and the ship struck the dreaded Cowloe rocks and foundered. He and his men, battling with tremendous seas, launched a boat, but this too was overturned, and Ralph, his son, his cousin and his crew were flung into the water. Flares from the foundering ship had warned the household ashore, and John Penrose came down from the manor house to Sennen cove. Standing there, in the darkness and the wind, he heard the cries of the stricken men and, it was later whispered, did nothing for them, but let them drown. Ralph, William, all the crew were lost. The only one to come ashore, mercifully unharmed, was his nephew, the heir, the lad of seven.

64

"Life changed at Penrose manor after that mournful night. John, appointing himself guardian of his nephew, behaved as if the property were his. The old quiet ways were over, and riotous living took their place. The fisherfolk in Sennen dreaded for the safety of their wives and daughters, who dared not stir from their doors when John Penrose was abroad. Fearing the sea himself he built a larger, stronger craft than ever his brother had owned, and manned it with a captain and crew whose reputation for evil living excelled even his own, so that now the name of Penrose was not connected with fair-trading but with piracy. On winter nights when the villains shunned the sea, John Penrose would invite the captain and his crew to drink with him at the manor, and wild would be the shouting and the laughter, and blazing the torch-lights and the lanterns, as the drunken inmates staggered about the courtyard and stumbled in the passages and hall.

"One winter snow fell upon Sennen, and rumour ran that wolves had been seen on the commons above Penrose. Half-crazed with excitement and drink, John Penrose bade his household go in search of them, while he and his boon companion, the skipper of the pirate vessel, stayed within doors, a bottle of brandy on the table between them.

"When the servants returned they called for their young master, the heir, to tell him that the wolves had vanished, but the boy was nowhere to be seen, neither in the house nor in the grounds outside. His uncle and the captain, too drunk to answer questions, murmured that the lad, having gone to join the hunt, would soon return. Once more the steward and the servants went out into the night, across the fields to the cliffs, even down to Sennen cove, where the orphaned boy so often wandered, musing upon his father's death. They found no trace of him, neither that night, nor in the light of morning, nor in the days to come. It was assumed that young Penrose, blinded perhaps by the driving snow, and missing his way, had fallen from a cliff into the sea, and drowned there amongst the rocks as his father had before him. The household mourned, but John Penrose, being full master at last, gave himself up to even greater folly than before, spent recklessly, gambled his heritage, and led his band of vagabonds about the countryside, putting the fear of death into all his neighbours. One thing was strange. He took an aversion to the captain of his ship, who, giving no explanation to anyone, relinquished his command and left the district.

"The following winter, on the anniversary of the boy's disappearance, between Christmas and New Year, John Penrose was carousing amongst his cronies when a stranger came into the courtyard of the house, and knocking upon the door asked for hospitality. The steward admitted him, for wanderers often begged shelter at these times, and his master, deep in his cups, ordered that the guest should be shown to his dead brother's room in the old wing. A fire was laid and kindled in the hearth and the steward brought food and drink, and as he placed them before the guest he admitted, shaking his head, that evil days had fallen upon the house. Strange things were seen and heard that never were before, and all since the young heir had been lost twelve months ago. The stranger listened in silence, if silence it could be called, for even in the old wing the sound of revelry came from the hall below.

"The steward left, bidding the guest goodnight. The stranger opened the window which gave on to the side-court and watched the revellers making merry because of the New Year to come, picking ivy, strewing it upon themselves and the cobbles, shouting how some of them would be wedded before the year was out. Suddenly one of them cried out in fright, pointing to the white wreaths of mist and fog rolling in towards them from the sea. One and all they ran back into the house and slammed the door, and the music and sounds of revelry ceased. The stranger waited, watching the rolling mist."

Here I was interrupted by my son. "You're making it up," he said.

"No," I said, "really, I'm not."

"You must be," he insisted. "You're bringing in the fog because of last time, when it came down on us after Madron Well."

66

"No," I told him, "it's coincidence. The fog is all part of the old story."

He grunted, disbelieving. "Well, anyway, go on."

"The fog came first," I continued, "and then, from the same direction, came a sound like the roaring of the sea, yet the sea was distant a mile or more, and the manor of Penrose set at the valley's head between the hills. The sound of the storm drew nearer, the roar of breakers upon the shore, the rattling of oars shipping into the row-locks, and the splintering of wood, and in a moment the breakers themselves tumbled upon the courtyard, bearing upon their crest a long boat filled with crying men, who called out in terror, 'Save us . . . Save us . . .' The sea was all about the house, curling and green, and the boat of a sudden overturned, spilling her crew, who with white faces and staring eyes sought to save themselves, and sank; but one man, lasting longer than his comrades, looked up at the window where the stranger stood and cried in a loud voice, 'William Penrose, arise and avenge the murder of your cousin's son!' Then all was still. There was no more storm and no more sea, no more anguish of drowning men. The court was cobbled as it had been before, the ivy strewn where the revellers had left it. The mist dis-solved.

"The stranger, William Penrose, for it was indeed he, the cousin, believed by all in Sennen to be drowned, passed his hand over his eyes. The memory of that terrible night came back to him. How he had dragged himself ashore and wandered, a vagrant, about the countryside unknown to any man, and finally taken ship to a distant land until some instinct within him made him seek out his home, as he had done that night.

"The words rang in his ears. 'Avenge the murder of your cousin's son!' He flung himself upon his bed to sleep, and while he slept it seemed to him that the voice of the young boy whispered in his ear, 'My uncle bade the captain murder me. I lie beneath the dead tree in the orchard. Dig, and you shall find me. Dig, and place my bones in Sennen churchyard. Dig, and give me peace at last.'

"When morning came William Penrose awoke, and seeking out the good steward in his quarters there revealed himself for whom he was, swearing the man to secrecy. He said nothing of the fearful revelations of the night before, for he wished first to find, if possible, the murderous captain who had killed his cousin's son. He traced him, after several days, to Plymouth, where the wretched fellow, unfit for further piracy or plotting, tortured by remorse and fear of discovery, lay dying in a lodging-house. When questioned he confessed all, admitting that it was not for gold only that he had killed the boy but because, as a young man, he had loved the child's mother, and when she had married Ralph the devil had entered his heart.

"There, on the lodging-house bed, the captain died, and William returned to his cousin's house. He found the master absent, for since the night of Christmas revelry, so the steward told him, John Penrose had fallen into a fit of melancholy, desiring neither drink nor company, nor had he been seen to smile or raise his head. Together, William and the steward went to the orchard. One tree, amongst the others, was naked white, the branches bare and pointing to the sky. They dug beneath it. Slowly, gently, they lifted the tangled remains of the once lovely boy, the clothes about him stained with blood and mould. They carried him by night to Sennen churchyard and laid him to Christian rest as he had desired, saying nothing to any member of the household, nor to the villagers, out of respect for the once honoured family name.

"When they returned to Penrose they found the door of the malthouse below the manor blowing wide, and entering they saw something swaying backwards and forwards from a beam. It was the body of John Penrose. He had hanged himself in sight of the blasted tree."

My son, intent upon navigation through the city of Truro, was brought to a stop by the traffic lights. "Is that the end?" he asked.

"For that branch of the family, yes," I answered. "William found the place so haunted still that he gave up his rights to it and went away forever, to the Holy Land, people said. There was a mortgage on the property and it was sold to somebody called Jones, who did some smuggling on the side himself. But either he or his descendants pulled most of the house down, and according to the *Parochial History of Cornwall* it's now a farm."

"What's the date of your *Parochial History?*"

I thought a moment. "About 1872," I said.

My son smiled, and we sped on towards Redruth and Camborne, to cross the river Hayle for West Penwith. I knew what he was thinking: the discovery in a library can turn to disenchantment in the field. But the risk is always worth the running, and at least the terrain cannot change, the contour of the hills, the cut of valleys. As we drove I considered, silently, how myth can weave itself into a story, borrowing a thread here, a thread there, and the product is never finally finished, for always a new hand will take delight in fashioning further patterns. Somewhere in the Penrose tale must have lain a seed of truth. Two brothers, the elder drowned, an ailing child standing between the younger one and the property: this was the basic story, bereft of embroidery.

We came to Sennen village, and, filling up with petrol, asked for the farmhouse of Penrose. We were directed to take a road inland towards the valley, where a gate would set us on the track to the farm. The countryside, if no longer quite as wild and barren as the old book had described it, was nevertheless windswept, and as we approached the valley excitement grew. We found the gate and motored up the track, no building yet in sight. There was a bank to the right of us, and beyond, winding through sunken fields, ran the stream. As we turned a bend in the track and climbed the hill we saw farm-buildings, in the distance, outlined against the sky.

We had found Penrose. We bumped our way forward, coming to rest on the crest of the hill in the immediate vicinity of the farm. Cow-sheds, lofts above them, lay to our right, and in front of us, enclosed on either side by old stone walls, one of them set about with little square recesses for the pigeons that had nested there in days gone by, stood the house itself. The roof was slated, the walls were granite, the chimneys tall and square. A replica of many a Cornish farmhouse of uncertain date, Georgian in all probability. No cobbled courtyards now, no spacious halls, no haunted bedrooms lurking

We had found Penrose.

above-stairs. Solid, comfortable, well kept, a television aerial upon the roof.

We climbed out of the car, and as we did so a man came from one of the buildings to our right. The owner of the farm in person. I apologised for trespassing, and told him briefly of our quest.

"Yes," he said, "they say the family of Penrose did live here once. But my people have had it for more than seventy years."

I murmured something about three or four hundred years before his father's birth, some old tale of murder and distress. His eyes showed interest. "I've heard that too," he said. "My son picked it up in school. In some book, you say? It may have been."

He let us wander. I cast my eye about for the malt-house with the open door where no malt-house stood now, then stared back again at the solid granite house, the neat clipped lawn beneath the windows. The walled court where the revellers had strewed ivy was now a yard for scratching hens. Was this where the sea swept, bearing drowning men? Somewhere behind the façade of the farmhouse I glimpsed an older, mediaeval dwelling, with a central hall within, a log fire burning on the hearth. The owner, John Penrose, was seated before it with the pirate captain, the brandy bottle between them, and in a room near by waited a frightened orphaned boy.

"The orchard," murmured my son, "ask about the orchard."

"Oh, yes," I said, following the farmer, "was there ever an orchard here?"

He turned and pointed to the valley whence we had come. "There was an orchard once," he said, "down there, close to the stream. Nothing left of it now."

We thanked him for his courtesy, and unwilling to trespass further we got back into the car, and drove downhill to the bank. Once out of sight of the farm we stopped the car and crept down the bank to look upon the marshy meadow where long ago the orchard grew. No cattle grazed beside the stream. The place was desolate. One solitary tree, no orchard seedling but an elm or oak, stood in mid-field, tall branches spread against the sky. We looked at each other, nodding, our sense of myth and legend satisfied.

"Do you think if we got spades and dug?"

"Three centuries too late."

As we crouched there in the hollow I thought I heard the sea, but Sennen and the cliffs were nearly two miles away. It must have been the wind. We got up, and climbed back again to the farm-track, taking a last look westward to Penrose upon the hill. Clouds, fore-telling rain before evening, were banking up against the sun, and the air that blew about us tasted salty, queer.

Chapter Six

THE HIGH COAST AND THE LIZARD

Kerrier, "the high coast," forms the southern grip of Cornwall's claw, its pincher probing the Channel at Lizard Point, while across the bay, in West Penwith, Gwennap Head stabs the Atlantic. The two Hundreds, Penwith and Kerrier, are in themselves near-peninsulas, the sea washing them on either side, and for this reason both have been notorious through the centuries for wrecks. In old days a ship under sail, caught in a sudden gale some miles offshore, could scarcely hope to avoid one or other of the pinching claws; and if the rocks at Lizard or Land's End did not break her back, then she would be driven into the open jaw of Mount's Bay, a lea-shore to all sou'westerlies, unless she could reach Penzance and shelter.

The "high coast" starts before Trewavas Head, and almost immediately close inshore of the curving bay lie the Megiliggar rocks, which destroyed many a vessel in days past, while on the cliffs at Methleigh are the graves of bodies washed in by the sea. It was not until 1830 that the member of Parliament for Bodmin, Mr. Davies Gilbert, introduced an Act into Parliament sanctioning the burial of persons washed up by the sea in consecrated ground in the nearest parish churchyard, the expenses to be paid out of the county rate. Until that time, no matter who it was that drowned, they found the nearest ditch or field as resting-place, or else were thrown back into the sea to seek another refuge down the coast. Sometimes a body became "sanded," that is to say, sunk in the moist sand and covered by it during a flowing-tide. The superstitious ashore would then declare that they saw corpse-lights flickering at night to mark the spot, or they would hear what was termed the "calling of the dead," the voices of the drowned seamen hailing their own names. Much of the fear of being shipwrecked came from the dread that Christian burial would be denied, and that, because of this, a seaman's ghost would always haunt the scene of death, forever restless. The same fear gripped the relatives ashore. A drowned father, brother, son became a menace in the night, eternally reproaching, and changed in a fearful way from the loved one he had been. Here is very ancient myth at work again, the belief of primitive peoples that the dead are to be feared unless, with due ritual, their bones are burnt or buried.

When the Reformation came, and Mass was no longer said over the bodies of the dead or for the souls of those departed, the Cornish people felt themselves bereft of consolation; frequently exposed, as the fisherfolk were, to death by drowning, their terror of such an end was all the greater, absolution seeming no longer theirs. Instinct made them turn to superstition; the old pagan longings surged within them. They saw lords of the manor, men they had hitherto respected, stripped of their estates and imprisoned, and this was baffling to the poorer people, suggesting that all authority had been overthrown. So it was that they began to have little regard for the property of others or the possessions of strangers. When times were hard and winters rough, a vessel cast up upon their shores was as good as a harvest, the cargo theirs for the gleaning. Hence the famous "wrecking" – often exaggerated, in essence true – that has given the Cornish coasts a bad name throughout history.

The rugged cliffs of West Penwith and Kerrier, thinly populated, the small fishing-villages, little more than hamlets clustered above highwater in the coves, were remote from the law and order which ruled inland. Weather-bound in winter, existing on a bare subsistence of salted fish, the inhabitants saw no evil in plundering a foundered ship if the contents helped to fill their bellies or put clothes upon their backs. Dead men told no tales, and a drowning man was as good as dead, more so if a stranger; but the Catholic conscience sought release in the legends of spirits and restless ghosts.

Today, and for some years past, Lizard Point has had to answer neither for crying seamen nor for ghosts. A lighthouse station warns all passing shipping to keep well distant from its still menacing shores. The rocks breaking surface beneath the point have a more ragged, deadly face than those beyond Land's End. They straggle in a thin black line, or hump themselves into whales' backs, and even in a moment of dead calm, with the still sea washing their sides in a caress, they hold potential danger, sharp teeth laid bare, malevolent and black.

The time to walk about the Lizard headland is in winter or early spring, when cafés are shuttered and colour-wash has not been put upon the bungalows to deck them for the season yet to come. Our Londoner, Walter White, who scrambled about the cliffs in 1854, found Lizard town "a poor scattered village, with one tavern recently built for the entertainment of visitors," and this he seems to have avoided, preferring to buy refreshments at "a little tenement facing the sea." He had walked from Cadgwith along the coast, where he had met with half a gale of wind (and this in summer) that nearly drove him headlong into the chasm known as the Devil's Frying-Pan. Cornwall above all counties, he remarked, appeared to be subjected to visitations from the Evil One. The landscape everywhere was dreary, dangerous, and a painful sense of loneliness stole over him. The Frenchman Alphonse Esquiros fared no better ten years later. A sudden storm surprised him, lightning flashed, thunder rolled, and he was obliged to seek shelter with a flock of frightened sheep lying huddled beneath monstrous blocks of stones.

Both these wayfarers, as well as Wilkie Collins the novelist, who rambled about the Lizard headland at much the same period, were haunted by a story of shipwreck and death connected with the spot called Pistol Meadow. This gruesome tale, difficult to envisage on a day of high summer in the tourist season, is not too hard to reconstruct on a late afternoon in February, or better still December, when the sea, a sullen grey, lashes the rocks, and the cliff paths are muddied with winter rains.

In the mid-eighteenth century a transport ship was wrecked on a reef off Lizard Point, and a couple of hundred corpses were washed ashore in the stony cove beneath the westward cliff. The Lizard people found them at low tide, jammed into rock crevices, tangled up in seaweed, half hidden under stones, and scattered near to the reef where the ship had foundered a great quantity of firearms, mostly pistols. Above the cove a rough meadow sloped to the cliffs, good for little except grazing, and here the people dug pits in which to bury the dead soldiers, carrying the bodies one at a time up the steep path from the cove. The task was hard, taking several days, and to the horror of the men who dug the pits and bore the bodies to them they found the shore invaded by packs of hungry dogs, appearing not only from their own neighbourhood but from the outlying country, all seeking to prey upon the drowned. But at last there was not a single body left upon the shore; each poor soldier lay with his fellows in the common graves above, and forever after the place was known as Pistol Meadow.

In after months, and even years, so it was said, the Lizard people shunned the companionship of dogs. They drove them from the district, and there was not a household for several miles about that cared to own one. Wilkie Collins was particularly struck by this phenomenon. He walked through farmyard after farmyard and heard no barking; there was never an animal upon its chain lying stretched outside a kitchen door, no puppy dragging upon a string. Their absence upon the Lizard headland and in the countryside near by confirmed to him in all its ugliness the full horror of the story.

Visiting the scene some hundred years or more after Wilkie Collins, I looked uneasily about me for the sight of a mangy cur loping towards the cliffs and being pelted with stones by village boys, but all was orderly. Near to the lighthouse a man, painting the inside of a café, pointed out Pistol Cove west of the point, but the meadow was more difficult to place, for the cliff walk above the cove was bounded with wire for safety's sake – there had been a recent fall of earth – and then the path wound to the left to the further head-land and a look-out hut beyond. Here was no meadow with sweet-smelling wild flowers and waving grass blowing peacefully over the mounds of the dead, as described by Wilkie Collins. The rough ground sloped directly to the cliff, intersected by a stream, the

Forever after the place was known as Pistol Meadow.

mounds I trod were natural hillocks sprouting gorse, until . . . could this be it?

A small enclosure, set about with stumpy willows grotesquely shaped by the prevailing wind, the ground hussocky and rough. The whole of the enclosure, if dug, would not have covered more than fifteen to twenty square feet. Some versions of the story talked of graves, others of pits. Pits, or one large trench, seemed the more likely. Perhaps, as Wilkie Collins said, wild flowers grew here once, and in his day, before the stumpy willows formed, the mound of the pit would have shown, now sunken with a century of winter rains. It was peaceful, untroubled, better than many another resting-place for sleeping soldiers.

Looking upon it, and then out to sea, I thought back some thirty-five years or more to a night spent in the Lizard hotel, perhaps that same "one tavern" mentioned by White the Londoner, and how I could not sleep because the lighthouse beam swept my window each minute. One, three, five, it was as if every other moment, with maddening persistence, someone entered the room and flooded it with light, then flicked it off again, while, as the night lengthened and the weather worsened, the foghorn boomed. Two hundred years ago there were no beacons and no warnings, and all the soldiers of the transport heard was the sound of the sea breaking on the reef, while they waited, huddled on the decks, for the first tearing crash as the vessel struck.

My memory took another leap back in time to the summer when, recovering from measles at the age of ten, and staying some three miles or so from Lizard Point, I taught myself to swim on Kennack sands. Or, rather, in a pool set beneath the cliffs, mysterious and shallow, yet deep enough to cover a child's hips. The water was always still, warm and inviting, while out upon the sands themselves the waves were high, too boisterous for my taste, and icy cold. My elder sister and my aunt jumped up and down in them, spray-washed, delighted, but to me, even then, the sea seemed cruel, demanding victims. I wanted no part of it. The pool was best.

Nor was it wise to wander very far, for a little boy, so we were told, had disappeared one day never to return, held by the quicksands. Not here at Kennack, my mother and my aunt hastily reassured us, but somewhere else in Cornwall, miles away. We doubted them. Quicksands were golden, more beautiful than other sands, hence their terrible temptation to the strayer. A child could run on them unheeding, barefoot, towards the sea, and suddenly one foot would sink, and then the other, down to his knees, his thighs, his chest, and

Kennack sands.

all about him the golden sands would start to tremble. The boy's father had been a publisher called Grant Richards. His house was set on the cliffs not far away, in a wild and tangled garden, both house and ground unkempt. The publisher did not live there any more, grieved by the loss of his son.

A dreadful curiosity led us to explore, the three of us pressing our faces against the window-panes. Nothing to see; but I knew he was not far, the running boy, bare-legged, in shorts, a shrimping-net over his shoulder, running, always running, towards the golden sands.

The past swung into the present, and I was back again on the rough turf of Pistol Meadow. Somehow the whole of Lizard Point and the adjoining cliffs and coves became too full of phantoms for my taste. I called to my son and we climbed back to the parking-place, bought ice-cream cornets with callous greed, and drove fast and furiously along the high road, westward once more. I wanted him to see the stretch of shore, whiter, firmer, even more golden than the quicksands where Grant Richards' boy had run half a century before, which, with no ill-repute but only beauty to enchant the wanderer, is set, miraculously, between lake and sea.

It is called the Loe Bar. The approach from the east is by way of a narrow lane descending steeply, unpractical, praise heaven, for a car.

The sea upon his left, and to his right the stiller waters of an inland lake.

The visitor must walk, and is rewarded for his pains by the sudden appearance of the sea upon his left, a whole wide sweep of bay, and to his right the darker, stiller waters of a broad inland lake. The high ridge of sand acts as a bridge between the two, and if the day is fine and the sun shining the effect is dazzling to the eye, the sea a brilliant blue breaking upon the bar, which in itself is gleaming white, and on the nearer side the ripple of fresh lake water, lapping the softer sand. No buildings mar the opposite hill, save for one house on the cliff road leading to the small harbour of Porthleven, and the rest is trees, sloping to the lake's edge. I cannot speak for summer, for such a picnic-spot must draw a thousand visitors, but in winter and spring the white sand is untrodden, like Crusoe's island, not even spattered by Man Friday's footprints.

In winter, after heavy rain, the streams rushing down from Helston fill the lake, which overflows and runs across the sand to meet the bar. Then, if the wind blows strongly and the tide is at the flood on the top of springs, the sea in turn sweeps forward to the bar, and the waters meet.

Whoever stands upon the strand at such a time must feel like Moses, waving the twelve tribes onward, while behind him come the galloping chariots of Pharaoh in pursuit. There is a channel cut today on the western side, allowing the lake waters to escape, and they tumble out of a gully in rushing turmoil, frothing and foaming as they find the sea. In old times this was not so. A curious custom prevailed. The lake and all the land adjoining it was owned – is still owned, for that matter – by the lord of the manor, whose house was on the western hill amongst the trees. The millers on the estate, with cottages near to the streams and the flooding lake, their livelihood threatened, would go to him bearing purses, each containing three halfpence, and presenting him with these purses would ask permission to cut a path through the bar between lake and sea, so permitting the flood to find its way seaward. The lord of the manor would give his consent, acceptance of the money being recognition of his rights, and then the millers would take their spades and shovels and go down to the beach and dig their trench. It was no great labour, for

They tumble out of a gully in rushing turmoil.

the lake waters, bursting to be away, soon thrust a passage in the oozing sand, and with a roar like thunder lake and ocean mingled.

They say, in the old books, that the sound of it could be heard for miles inland, and it was like a battle between giants to see which would prevail upon the other, the brackish flooding waters or the angry sea. The lake, with all the persistence of the winter rains within it, was the conqueror. The tide would turn, the sea retreat, taking with it a great muddied, yellow stream, staining its surface far and wide into the bay. The battle continued with each ebb and flow, until the lake sank once more to its customary tranquillity, no longer in full spate, and the incoming sea, less furious than before, closed the channel, building up the ridge of sand. The bar formed a barrier again, dividing lake and sea, until another winter came.

We walked backwards and forwards upon the strand, picturing the scene, and turning to the lake saw a small sailing-yacht put out from somewhere near the northern wooded slopes, and beat about in idle grace. The lord of the manor was in possession still.

Chapter Seven

THE CORNISH GENTRY

THE first Earl of Cornwall was Robert de Moriton, half-brother to William the Conqueror, and afterwards the earldom passed down at the whim of the monarch to whichever of his near relatives, legitimate or otherwise, he thought fittest to inherit it; until Edward III, that wise and far-seeing king, converted the earldom to a dukedom and invested his son, the Black Prince, with the title. "By putting a Wreath on his Head, a Ring on his Finger, and Verge or Rod into his Hand; ever since which Time it has been settled and agreed, That the eldest Son of the King, who is Heir to the Crown, shall be Earl of Cornwall, and by a special Act of Parliament made in that Case, he is presumed to be of an Age as soon as he is born, so that he may claim Livery and Seisin of the said Dukedom the same Day he is born, and ought by Right to obtain it, as if he had fully completed the Age of 21 years."

This was the intention, but eldest sons have died and younger brothers become invested in their turn. Or the inheritance has been handed down in other ways, as when the House of Stuart departed, to be succeeded by the Hanovers, and George, Prince of Wales, took over the dukedom by letters patent.

Neither the earls nor the dukes of Cornwall – with the exception of Richard, brother of Henry III, and his son Edmund, both of whom dwelt from time to time at Dunheved Castle, Launceston, and Restormel Castle, Lostwithiel – have ever lived on their estates. Therefore no great tradition grew up around a resident duke whose castle or manor would have become a hub of power, with courtiers and nobles vying for their master's favour and Court influence

Launceston Castle.

spreading throughout the duchy. Had it been so, the history of Cornwall would have been different, more turbulent, perhaps. Absent rulers give their subjects a greater chance to become self-sufficient, to choose their way of life, and the Norman families who came over to England with the Conqueror and settled down in lands west of the Tamar, though they did not forget their proud descent, became one with the indigenous and more impoverished Cornish, deciding for themselves which side to take when battles raged elsewhere.

The Black Death brought devastation to the people, the French wars prosperity – at any rate to the Cornish ports. During the Wars of the Roses most of the leading gentry were for the House of Lancaster – Edward Courtenay of Boconnoc, Sir Thomas Arundell of Lanherne, Richard Edgecumbe of Cotehele, John Treffry of Place House in Fowey; but Sir Henry Bodrugan, of Bodrugan near Meva-

Restormel Castle, Lostwithiel.

gissey, declared his support for the House of York, and was rewarded for his loyalty by Richard III with the grant of lands belonging to his neighbours. But the Yorkist cause was lost at Bosworth Field, Henry VII was proclaimed King, and Sir Henry fled the country, never to return. His house, or rather the site of it, is now a farm, and near to the cliff's edge is the spot called Bodrugan's Leap, where the knight is said to have escaped pursuit by jumping his horse from cliff to shore, and so away, presumably by boat to France.

Henry VII rewarded his Lancastrian supporters, and the gentlemen of Cornwall were once more secure. Some remnant of Yorkist loyalty remained nevertheless in the hearts of lesser men, blacksmiths, tinners, laywers, hard hit by taxes levied for a war against the Scots; and in June of 1497 a band of these courageous Cornishmen marched through Devon and Somerset as far as Blackheath south of London, armed with crowbars and picks, in the vain hope that the

King would listen to their protestations. But there was an army of ten thousand men waiting at Blackheath, who made short work of them. The two leaders of the Cornish party, the lawyer Flamank and the blacksmith Joseph, were hanged, drawn and quartered at Tyburn ten days after the so-called battle, their followers having either deserted or been killed.

In September they rallied again, when Perkin Warbeck declared himself to be the younger of the two Princes in the Tower, believed to have been murdered (though he never said how he had survived), and landed near Land's End, in Whitesand Bay. Once more the rebel band set off for London, after proclaiming Perkin Richard IV at Bodmin. The Cornish gentry, scenting disaster, stayed within their estates, and the six thousand men who marched on Exeter had nobody but their bogus prince to rally them. Repulsed at Exeter they went on to Taunton, where Perkin's nerve deserted him, and under cover of night he abandoned his Cornish army, who, angry and disheartened, were forced to surrender to King Henry. Taxes were levied in every Cornish parish to pay the fine demanded as the price of rebellion.

It was fifty years before Cornishmen crossed the Tamar again in open revolt, after the Act of Uniformity had been passed in January of 1549, abolishing the old Latin Mass and substituting the new English service. The people were outraged. Already they had seen priories and monasteries stripped, their contents given to enrich those members of the gentry – and they were in the majority – who favoured the Reformation; but the forbidding of the Mass was the final straw. They did not understand the new Prayer Book, and preferred the old Latin with its familiar sound to this mouthing in English, which some of them could not even speak. A few days after Whitsun, when the new Prayer Book was first used, many Cornish parishes were in uproar, and this time they had a member of their own gentry to lead them, Humphry Arundell, related to the Arundells of Lanherne in Pyder, one of the oldest families in Cornwall, fanatically Catholic.

Rebellion against the new Prayer Book was launched at Bodmin

The siege of Exeter.

under Humphry Arundell's command, and as the rebels crossed the
Tamar they were joined by Catholic supporters in Devon. Exeter was
besieged for five weeks, and Catholic hopes began to rise, for if
Exeter fell many more Devonians might rally to their cause. It was not
to be. The garrison at Exeter was reinforced, the siege was raised, the
Cornish Catholics, after a stout resistance, were beaten, and
Humphry Arundell was finally captured and taken to London, where

he suffered the same fate as the lawyer and the blacksmith fifty years before.

The Cornish Catholics were crushed, one or two priests were hanged, the people lost their Mass, and if they did not go to church they were sent to gaol. The Mass was restored to them briefly under Mary Tudor, but when Elizabeth ascended the throne the new English Prayer Book was thrust upon the Cornish once again, this time forever. The big landowners were firmly Protestant, and only the Arundells remained strong for the Catholic faith. Failure to attend the parish church cost Sir John Arundell some £20 a month, a large sum for those days. He and his near relatives celebrated Mass in their homes, and priests were harboured in the disguise of guests; this was the moment when secret rooms were built, "priests' holes" as they were called at a later date.

When war broke out between England and Catholic Spain the Cornish gentry proved their loyalty to their Protestant monarch. Sir Richard Grenville of Stowe in Stratton won immortality when he fought fifty-two Spanish galleons from the deck of his small ship *Revenge*, and died in so doing. This, for the Cornish gentlemen, was their finest hour, religious bickering forgotten in the struggle against a common enemy; but they divided once again in Stuart days, when the Civil War raged up and down the length and breadth of England, spreading to the Cornish countryside. It was not a people's war, and what the tinners, the fishermen and other labouring men thought of it history has not recorded. Those whom the leading gentry led into battle were tenants from their own estates, farmers, labourers, wood-men, household servants, all of whom could be relied upon for loyal devotion to whichever side their master had espoused. Many a gallant action was fought between 1642 and 1646 by these Cornish gentlemen, tales of which are told down to the present time; and many a bloody skirmish, too, for opportunity was taken to settle old scores and private jealousies.

The Grenville brothers of Stowe – Sir Bevil and Sir Richard, grand-sons of Grenville of the *Revenge* – epitomised all that was best and worst in the Cornish character. Both had inherited the lion-hearted

AN° DÑI · 1571 ·
ÆTATIS · SVÆ ·
· 29 ·

Sir Richard Grenville.

Sir Bevil Grenville.

courage of their grandfather, but it was to Richard that the great man bequeathed his ruthlessness. Bevil, the elder brother, was a land-owner, a devoted husband and father, who asked for nothing better in life than to administer his estates with fairness to his family and his tenants; but when the Civil War broke out he was among the first to seize his sword, arm his followers and declare for the King's cause. The first engagement on Cornish soil was fought below Boconnoc on Bradock Down, and so furious was the charge which Bevil led that the Parliament troops were routed and fled in disorder. Sir Bevil had his tenants drawn up in solemn prayer before the battle, dressed in his blue and silver livery, and he asked for God's blessing upon King Charles and all who served him. Then with his standard-bearer, Tony Paine, a great giant of a man some seven feet tall, waving the standard bearing a griffin's head upon it, Bevil Grenville led his people down the hill, shouting as they went, "A Grenville . . . A Grenville . . . ," cutting the enemy to pieces as they charged.

There is a stone monument on Bradock Down today marking the spot. The downland lies beside the main road from Liskeard to

There is a stone monument on Bradock Down marking the spot.

Lostwithiel, and the slope, overgrown with bush and sapling, seems a small place to have known, three hundred and twenty-odd years ago, the tramping of horse, the cries of dying men and the stench of battle. This was in January of 1643, and in May Bevil Grenville repeated his assault, this time at Stratton near his home, close to the Tamar's source, and with the other Royalist leaders drove the enemy out of Cornwall.

The lull was temporary. In July he led his Cornishmen to join the main Royalist army in an attack on Bath, where a fierce battle took place on Lansdowne ridge, held by the enemy. Bevil Grenville, thinking to repeat his victory at Stratton, led his men uphill to seize the guns. He fell, mortally wounded. Thereupon his standard-bearer, Tony Paine, seized Sir Bevil's young son John, a boy barely fourteen, and clapped him upon the dying man's horse, and the boy, the tears smarting in his eyes, brandished his father's sword and rode in the enemy's pursuit. This was the sort of action, instinctive, gallant, that made the name of Grenville memorable.

Bevil's brother, Sir Richard, was a man of different calibre, a professional soldier who had fought in Germany and Ireland. With mercenary cunning he accepted £600 from the Parliamentary leaders, and then went off and joined the forces of the King. Brutal, ruthless, a tremendous disciplinarian and an able tactician hated by his enemies, feared and sometimes mistrusted by his friends, he soon became exasperated by the careless methods of his co-commanders. They were slow in decision, so he thought, not swift enough in pursuit; they went about the business of war as if it were a game instead of a process of extermination. No quarter asked or given was his motto, and after he had helped to lure the Parliament army into Cornwall, with the intention of cutting them to pieces in the peninsula or forcing them into the sea, he lived up to his maxim.

It might have been, had the other Royalist leaders listened to him, that the King's cause would have fared better than it did. Trapped in the neck of land between Fowey and Par, the Parliament forces under the Earl of Essex fought a hopeless battle at Castle Dor, site of King Mark's fortress; but in the misty rain Essex escaped to Fowey, and so to Plymouth in a fishing-boat, while others, under cover of night, rode eastward to the Tamar. And in the following year, 1645, the tide turned against the Cornish Royalists. The new leader of the Parliament forces, General Fairfax, was a far abler man than Essex. Grenville, resentful and fuming that he was not given supreme Royalist command, refused to obey the orders of his superior officer Lord Hopton, and was arrested by his own side. Fairfax pushed west and crossed the Tamar. It was the beginning of the end. He was in Bodmin by March of '46, and Hopton's forces were driven south to Truro.

In April Sir Arthur Basset of Tehidy surrendered St. Michael's Mount, the fortress island in Mount's Bay, but Sir John Arundell of Trerice held out at Pendennis fort until mid-August, a glorious show of courage and endurance. Sir Richard Grenville had meanwhile escaped to France. Whether he returned to take part in the abortive, quickly suppressed uprising in '48 is unlikely ever to be proved, but he declared himself always to be "The King's General in the West," and died, embittered and alone, in Holland in 1659, a year before the Restoration. Quarrelsome, unloved like his brother Bevil, save by his own men who would have followed him to death, Richard Grenville was a professional, and knew that the odds were heavy against the gallant but unco-ordinated amateurs on his own side. In England's and Cornwall's Civil War the amateurs struggled in a losing cause: it was the professionals who won.

During the Commonwealth some of the great estates had changed hands. John St. Aubyn, a Parliament supporter, held St. Michael's Mount instead of Arthur Basset. Francis Godolphin of Godolphin Hall went into exile, along with John Grenville, Sir Bevil's son. The Trelawnys of Trelawne were imprisoned and the Arundells fined. Johnathan Rashleigh of Menabilly was ruined and his home destroyed, so that only the outer walls remained standing. When the Restoration came in 1660, fortunes and estates were given back to their former owners, but the main body of the Cornish gentry, and the people with them, were weakened and impoverished, and from this time forward the great events of history passed them by. There were

The Rashleighs own Menabilly.

fortunes to be made by some in tin, a small amount of affluence for others in the enlarging and improvement of their estates, but the majority settled down to the life and pursuits of quiet country squires, busying themselves during the succeeding centuries with parochial and other matters, returning Members for Parliament, becoming sheriffs, magistrates, farmers, landscape gardeners, good and worthy men of no outstanding brilliance, the fires in their bellies quenched.

Certain houses fell into decay; others, rebuilt or restored, belong to descendants of their former owners, or are rented to tenants. The interested can visit some and peer at others from a distance, or poke about amongst the ruins where a house no longer stands. The Edge-cumbe house of Cotehele is National Trust, and so is Anthony where the Carew-Poles live. St. Michael's Mount is in St. Aubyn hands, Lanhydrock with the Agar-Robartes – the three last all Parliament men in the Civil War – their properties also now owned by National Trust. Vyvyans own Trelowarren, Rashleighs Menabilly, both

The fine old farmhouse of Stowe Barton stands above the site of the two Grenville homes.

Royalist supporters in the past. Treffrys are still in Place House at Fowey, but the Trelawnys have gone from Trelawne, Bassets have disappeared from Tehidy, now a hospital, and the Godolphins have gone from Godolphin Hall.

There are no more Arundells, and no more Grenvilles. These two families, the proudest and the most famous amongst the Cornish gentry, became extinct in Cornwall, the name passing to other branches east of Tamar. The curious and the nostalgic, desiring to wander where the Grenvilles once rode, hawked and hunted, can first drive to Kilkhampton church and look upon their sculptured monuments, then turn coastward towards Coombe, where the fine old farmhouse of Stowe Barton stands above the site of the two Grenville homes. Across the road are the foundations of the great house that John Grenville, son of Bevil, built over the remains of his father's dwelling when he was created Earl of Bath after the Restoration. This was pulled down after his death, and today there is little left of terraces and gardens but the old encircling walls. The coast and

the high cliffs are very near, and the clean, sharp air blows upon
them from the Atlantic

Leaving the Grenville territory in Stratton Hundred and continu-
ing down the north coast through Lesnowth and Trigg until we cross
the Camel estuary into Pyder, we can catch up with the same period
of history once again, and look upon the homes of the Arundells.
Trerice, three miles from Newquay, is one of the finest Tudor manor
houses in the county, and belongs today to the National Trust.
Lanherne, some eight miles to the north, seat of the Arundells from
the thirteenth century until it fell into decay when the male line died
out in 1701, lies in St. Mawgan village, and has been a Carmelite
convent since 1794.

It is fitting that this house, which had been the home of the
Catholic Arundells for five centuries, should have passed into the
care of Catholic nuns. The manner of its passing is worth recording.
The last Sir John's great-granddaughter, who had inherited the
property but did not live there, married a distant kinsman, the
seventh Baron Arundell of Wardour, thus uniting her branch of the
family with his. When the Toleration Act of 1781 permitted Catholics
to worship as they pleased without fines or persecution, in their own
chapels, it became easier for persons of the Catholic faith to dispose
of their property as they wished; and when a party of English
Carmelite nuns fled from Antwerp during the French Revolution and
came to London, the eighth Baron Arundell of Wardour presented
them with the old Cornish manor of Lanherne. On September 10,
1794, the Mother Prioress, Elizabeth Maddocks, with twelve nuns
and three lay sisters, entered the Arundell home. Some three years
later the final repairs were completed to the house, and the Carmelite
Sisters have now been in residence for over a hundred and seventy
years.

The façade of Lanherne, behind which lies the presbytery occupied
by the resident priest, looks much as it must have done when the
great Arundells called it home. Beyond, encircled by walls and
garden, is the enclosed convent, to which the outsider cannot penetrate. It is possible to enter the presbytery by arrangement, to mount

96

One of the finest manor houses in the county.

the stairway to the visitors' room and speak with the gracious Irish Prioress, separated from her guests by a double grille, and to attend one of the Offices in the chapel alongside the building. To do so is an unforgettable experience. It is not the austerity of enclosure, nor the monotony of day by day, that impresses the layman, but the atmosphere of warmth and welcome, peace and happiness within these walls, where thirteen nuns, like their many predecessors, have dedicated themselves to God and to a life of prayer.

Close by is St. Mawgan church, where the Arundells worshipped in days gone by, with its village in the valley near at hand, and the whole is permeated, in a moving and very real fashion, by this same atmosphere that rises from Lanherne itself, hallowed by centuries of good and faithful men and women. The feuds of the historic past are no more; flights and persecution, the wrangles of inter-Christian rivalry, all are forgotten. The countryside may change, big airfields spread on the high ground where Arundells once rode, small harbours turn to tourist towns, but Lanherne remains what it has always been for those who care for it and have long memories, the centre of a vanished Catholic Cornwall.

Chapter Eight

THE TINNERS

LONG before the ancestors of the Cornish gentry crossed over to England with William the Conqueror, and later rode west of Tamar into Cornwall to settle there; long before Arthur, Gorlois and Mark were Kings, and Tristan loved the Queen Iseult; long before Saxons wrought havoc and Romans built roads; back in the Bronze Age, some 1800 years B.C., the tinners were at work in Cornwall. Those first explorers from the Mediterranean lands who settled around the river Hayle and in West Penwith discovered the secret, or brought it with them – the secret being that the mixture of sand and stone washed down in the streams from the granite hills was a precious ore, tin, which, blended with the copper ore that they found in Ireland, turned into bronze. From this weapons were forged. Domestic uses came later, the lining of pots and pans, the making of cups, plates, bells – tin had a hundred uses; but in those early days, and for many centuries afterwards, the ore was sought because of the transformation into bronze when mixed with copper, and because, in the whole of Europe, the place with the largest deposits of this natural ore was the peninsula of Cornwall.

These early tinners worked in the open, amongst the rocks and furze, "streaming" the tin from the rock face where the veins of ore were exposed. Then the lighter waste was washed away from the gravel, and the heavier stones pounded into grain and taken to the furnace for smelting.

The Romans and the Saxons brought their own skill and knowledge to what was already a flourishing industry, but it was not until the twelfth century, in the reign of Richard I, that a code of laws was

The early tinners worked in the open, amongst the rocks and furze.

drawn up for the tinners. This was the first Charter for the Stannaries, as the industry came to be called. It laid down officially that the tinners could search for tin and work it, as had been their privilege from earliest times, in any waste land. The lord of the manor who owned the land would receive his toll, but apart from this he could not interfere in any way. This immediately established the tinner as his own master. He could dig where and how he liked. If the ore was forthcoming the profit was his; if there was none he was the loser.

The knowledge that he was his own master and obeyed no rules but those laid down in the Charter – watched over by the Warden of the Stannaries – put the Cornish tinner in a unique position amongst his fellow-men. He was not a serf, servant or hired labourer, but a free artisan. The tinners had their own Parliament, and their own Stannary courts for settling disputes. The sole tax was upon the tin itself, and this was strictly enforced by Stannary law, ensuring that all tin, once it was smelted, had to be taken to a coinage town.

There were four of these towns, Helston and Truro in the west, Lostwithiel and Liskeard in the east. Here the tin was weighed and taxed before the Officers of the Crown, then stamped with the Duchy arms. Afterwards it would be sold to the foreign traders; but the profits went to the tinners. These assemblies in the coinage towns, four times a year, were great occasions, sometimes lasting for as long as twelve days, with Midsummer Coinage the biggest festivity of all, giving an excuse for every sort of celebration.

The tinners still worked in the open, up on the moors amongst the granite or along the river banks, using pick and shovel, changing their ground as the stream deposits became exhausted. The "streamer" would take a lease or "set" from the landowner, generally for a year at a time, paying him either an agreed sum or a proportion of the tin found. He would work the set with members of his own family and, as he prospered, employ men to work with him. When the tin had been washed it was carried by pack-horse to the nearest blowing-house, for smelting, and the "blower" would rent his land from the landowner just as the tinner did.

A one-time tinner's cottage, St. Day.

Sometimes the set would be at a considerable distance from the hamlet or village where the tinners lived, and then they would build themselves moor-houses up on the waste land near to their work. These moor-houses were bare and sparse, one long windowless room where the men ate and slept, with a hearth on which they could burn turf and furze, and straw or heather on the floor to stretch themselves upon at night. In winter the days would be hard beyond belief, with a strong wind driving the rain across the moors and darkness setting in by half-past four. If the food they had brought with them ran short, they could trap rabbits or shoot wild-fowl, plover, woodcock, duck, that came to feed beside the pools and marshes amongst the heather and the scrub; then, in the smoke-filled atmosphere of their rough shelter, the tinners sat huddled beside the fire, telling each other legends of days past.

102

The cairns on the high moors were said to be haunted by the spirits of dead tinners, come to their death by misadventure, and later, when pick and shovel were used underground, tunnels and burrows dug and shafts sunk, and the tinners worked below the surface as miners, these creatures became distorted into evil spirits no more than three feet high, with squinting eyes and mouths from ear to ear. Whether they were ghosts or living no one could say, but the underworld was theirs, and the tin also, and to disturb one of them at work would bring bad luck. Men came across their tools in clefts of rock, small axes such as a gnome would fashion, sharp-edged and neatly turned. The name the tinners gave to them was "knackers," derived, it is thought, from the strange knocking and tapping heard when the miners first went underground, but that keen scholar Charles Henderson held the theory that originally the word was Anglo-Saxon for "Nicor", meaning an underworld fairy or water-sprite. This may well be, yet in later centuries the knacker was no benevolent water-imp but a little gnarled old man, hideous and ill-formed, with a head too big for his body, hung about with red or greying hair. The knackers went about in groups, changing shape or vanishing into smoke when a tinner drew near to them, and sometimes, for sheer devilry, turned into black buck-goats that grinned and scampered. When there were earth-falls underground, or water flooded in a pit and a man was drowned, it was always the work of the knackers, seeking revenge.

Tin-mining beneath the surface did not start until the middle of the fifteenth century, and as shafts were sunk deeper and tunnels grew longer so the work became harder and more dangerous, and knacker legends spread far and wide to every mine. Nothing was more conducive to superstition than the long tunnels in which a miner had to crawl or stand, half bent, his candle fixed to the brim of his hat, staying often as long as eight hours underground in hot and stagnant air.

"Unsavourie Damps doe here and there distemper their heads," wrote Carew in the *Survey of Cornwall* in Tudor days, but it was not only their heads that became distempered, whether with the foul air or the devilry wrought by the knackers. Their troubles grew in equal measure with the increased costs of working tin. Timber, ropes, candles, the sinking of shafts, the shoring-up of earth, the danger to life and limb, these were the anxieties of miners who worked underground instead of streaming in the open air.

The middle-man now came upon the scene, merchants who would loan the tinners money; or the more affluent amongst the tinners themselves, those who had struck it lucky and found a rich lode, would act as money-lenders in their turn. The landowner, too, began to realize that there was more in it for him than the mere leasing of a site. If he formed a company himself, and employed his own mining team, a fortune might be made or lost – it was worth the gamble. Sir William Godolphin of Godolphin Hall was one of these, and in the sixteenth century and later the Godolphins owned the richest tin land in all Cornwall. The Bassets of Tehidy, the St. Aubyns of the Mount were other families who grew rich in tin, the estates of all three spread about the tin-bearing grounds of Kerrier and Penwith.

The ordinary working miner, clinging to his independence, still preferred to work on "tribute" – that is to say, receive a share of the yield from the mine, rather than a fixed wage – and while this made for a sturdy pride in his own work, and independence, it also spelt insecurity, for a stream or mine that had been rich in ore one year might fail altogether the next, and the miner be without employment.

If times were bad, which was particularly the case during the latter part of the seventeenth and eighteenth centuries, when the price of tin fluctuated, the plight of the tinners became serious. Many of them came so near to starving that they used to band together and march on the nearest market-town, breaking into the merchants' houses in search of corn. There would be riots in Padstow, riots in Truro and Redruth, and the military would be called in to quell them; and just as in pre-revolutionary France rumours spread about the countryside of brigands and desperadoes breaking into the homes of law-abiding people, so in Cornwall the ordinary folk, farmers, shopkeepers and

104

the like, went about in fear of the tinners, who were held responsible for any disturbance, any breaking of the peace.

The tinners, so it was said, were a race of violent men who would stop at nothing, waylay travellers by night and beat them senseless, raid poultry-houses and barns, break doors and windows, set wrecking parties upon the cliffs with lanterns to lure ships to their doom and plunder them. These legends were founded on a reality of near starvation and the spirit of independence that made them different. They were, in fact, a race, not of violent men but of individualists, making their own terms when they streamed or dug for tin, beset by no ring of employers as in other industries; and this was mistrusted by those who had not the courage to do likewise. Even the tinners' festivals, customs, pastimes, were either feared or frowned upon as being un-Christian; hurling, wrestling, cock-fighting were the sports of violent men, leading to excess, to drunkenness and bloody fights.

"The common people," it was reported, "are a very strange kind of being, half savages at best."

The start of the nineteenth century, and the industrial revolution in the rest of the country, saw a boom in Cornish tin. Roads improved, foundries and engineering works were built, pumping-engines were driven by steam, and "foreigners from up-country" began to get a controlling interest in the mines, copper as well as tin, the vast paraphernalia of a capitalist set-up taking over from the former venturers. In spite of this change and expansion, the old spirit of camaraderie remained amongst the miners themselves. There were no class distinctions. The adventurers, as the shareholders were called, the mine captains or overseers, the pursers who looked after the finances, the local owners, all sat together at the monthly or quarterly meetings, and these occasions were made into festivals. A new engine would be installed like the launching of a ship, with flags flying and bands playing, the engine christened with a bottle of port. Each individual mine became the centre of the community, men, women, children all taking part in the work; but while fortunes came to the adventurers and the lucky landowners, the miners themselves had small share now in any profits, working long hours for low wages, so great was the competition to be employed at all.

They had come a long way from the days of their forebears who had streamed in the open on the moors, but their courage and endurance were as great as ever; mining was in their blood and they desired no other occupation. Disease took its toll. The average life-span of a miner working underground was forty-seven years, if he survived the all-too-frequent accidents; and when he came to the surface to end his days in an overcrowded cottage, spitting black dust, existing on a diet of potatoes and barley gruel, there was no trade union to look after him, no governmental agency or private benefactor to espouse his cause.

By the middle of the nineteenth century there were some fifty thousand of them working the mines, both tin and copper, for Cornwall was now the largest copper-producing district in the world, producing two-thirds of the entire supply. The mines were no longer concentrated in west Cornwall, in Penwith, Kerrier and Pyder, but sprawled eastward, covering the county. Lanescott was the largest, and Caradon Copper mine, north of Liskeard, on the borders of East and West Wivel, alone employed four thousand people. The boom reached its peak by the late Sixties, and then the bottom began to fall out of the market. Copper had been found by Lake Superior, tin in Malaysia, labour and production costs were lower there than in Cornwall, it no longer paid the landlords or the adventurers to risk their money in the west country. The great days were over. Companies folded up. Mines closed down. Hundreds, then thousands, of tin and copper miners found themselves out of work, without hope of employment. Production of copper alone fell from 160,000 tons to less than 500, and there was no alternative to starvation for the miners but mass emigration. A third of the mining population left Cornwall before the end of the century, taking their skill to other continents, to America, South Africa, Australia, while back at home their mining towns and villages were left unpeopled, the mines themselves deserted, no smoke coming now from the tall chimney-stacks, no sound of engines in the pumping-houses, the

The great Caradon Copper Mine, north of Liskeard.

land about them reverting once more to barren waste and scrub.

A brief revival came in the first part of the twentieth century and during the two world wars, but by then there were only four mines left, and today but two, Geevor in St. Just, South Crofty in Camborne. What the future holds for the Cornish mining industry no one can foretell. Other companies are prospecting, but British backing will be needed if Canadians and Americans are not to be first in the field. Tin and copper are still here beneath the soil awaiting new adventurers, new prospectors. Whether Cornishmen themselves are willing today to go underground like their forefathers, working perhaps for "tribute," a share in profits, as the old streamers did, and so have a stake in their own mine with all the pride and courage that go with such a venture, is something they can only answer for themselves.

The tinners of the past were an essential part of Cornwall, hunters, seekers, spending themselves in the unending quest for treasure underground. There is no difficulty in finding where they lived and worked. The chimney-stacks, naked against the sky, the ivy-covered engine-houses, the slack-heaps at the foot still gritty black – these are everywhere, glimpsed from a main road or a by-lane, crowded thickly in the mid-west belt of Kerrier and Penwith. Here possibly they are less easy to distinguish from foundries and factories in production, the Camborne–Redruth area being still the industrial belt; but strike north-eastwards to the coast near St. Agnes Head, or elsewhere, and you become aware suddenly of these lonely emblems of a once-crowded past. The names of the mines have a homely ring – Wheal Rose, Wheal Kitty, Wheal Harriet, Cook's Kitchen, Wheal Harmony, Wheal Fortune – somehow suggesting a vivid picture of the men who worked them, looking upon their mine as seamen do their ship, eternally "she" to be praised or cursed.

The trackways to the mines are overgrown, sometimes impassable, but if you hack your way through the brambles and come to an engine-house, and look about you, these places have all the beauty and the sadness that Nature gives to ruins. Perhaps they seemed ugly once, bare as electric pylons do today, smoke from the tall

Opposite: *The tinners of the past were an essential part of Cornwall.*

chimneys fouling the air, and instead of present silence the chug of machinery, the monotonous throb-throb of the pump. At early morning, after midday and again at evening, the bell would sound for the change of shift, and the roadways, now so full of weeds and bramble, would echo to the tread of men coming to work, while from underground to the shaft-heads climbed their fellows due for relief, clothes stained with mud and clay, a candle-stump fixed to their hard-brimmed hats.

More spectacular than the small inland mines are the chimneys and engine-houses of those built above the sea, perched like the nests of eagles. Botallack, near Cape Cornwall in West Penwith, has an almost eerie grandeur, set on a peak of rock with the Atlantic foaming at its base. Here, in old days, the subterranean workings extended below the sea-bed itself, several fathoms deep, and although no tragedy occurred the miners were forever aware of the ocean above their heads, the sinister roar of waves breaking against

A view of Botallack Mine, 1822.

E.T. ARCHIVE.

the distant cliffs, the seeping of salt-water into the rock crannies where they worked. This rock was their only protection from sudden death by drowning, the hot moist air about them made breathing difficult, and equally hard was the steep ascent by ladders to the cliffs when their shift was done, climbing perhaps at night through the pitch-black darkness, and in winter a full gale blowing.

Wheal Cotes on St. Agnes Head, if hardly as precariously steep, has the same stupendous beauty. The headland, now National Trust and unmarred by later building, is wild and bare, save for the bleak walls of the engine-house, standing like a defaced cathedral against the sky, while beneath it a solitary chimney-stack, formidable as a dark tower, frowns down upon the sea. Here it is not so easy to imagine the line of men climbing from their toil to the grassland and the open air. The site has more the drama of old legend, of days even before the miner hewed his way into rock and stone. This chimney surely never belched forth smoke, those walls never housed an engine's throbbing power. They stood for something outside time, like the tombs on the moorlands of West Penwith; memorials to daring and to courage, to the spirit of the miner himself, undefeated in adversity and loss, braving the centuries past, the centuries to come, symbols of a Cornish heritage.

Chapter Nine

RELIGION AND SUPERSTITION

RELIGION, to the Cornish, is bred in the bone, taking varying forms through successive generations. The first settlers, like most Mediterranean peoples, worshipped the Earth Mother, the fertility goddess who brought life to the world. The granite rocks and stones thrown up by nature in a million million years were her handiwork. Beneath them she presided, mysterious and dark, having power over all things inanimate and living.

The Celtic races brought a different cult, sky-gods, sun-gods, spirits of trees and woodlands, predominantly male, harbingers of the monotheistic God to come. Christianity made a perfect combination of the two opposing forces, male and female.

Then the holy men who came in droves from Ireland and Wales, baptising the Cornish, became saints in their turn, revered in their lifetime, petitioned after death. The pagan streams and wells were re-dedicated in their name, the hermits' cells turned into chapels. Churches were built, and the whole ecclesiastical order came into being. The Cornish accepted this with due reverence and obedience, yet underlying all conformity was a deep sense of superstition, half wondering, half afraid, a reliance on the old magic that had never died away.

Spells, charms, curses, wishes, these things sometimes had more power than prayer. Certain birds were baleful, certain animals malign. The dead were not in purgatory, or in their graves, but often wandered in the hills or called from the sea. The elderly were witches, the young were changelings. Knackers hammered and halloed from the mines, piskies, the household fairies, discomforted

The granite rocks and stones were her handiwork.

the home within, spoiling the foodstuff, turning the milk sour. No priest, no man of God, had control over these beings. They came and went at will, and it was safer to placate them, or to cast a counter-spell.

When the Reformation came and the mystique of the Mass was taken from the Cornish people, images forbidden, incense and holy water banished from the churches, they sought consolation in a greater dependence upon magic than before. If the Reformed church could not satisfy their deep emotional need, and the old Catholicism with its ritual was unlawful and men could hang and burn for practising it, then unconscious longing turned to an older cult, age-long memory stirred, and the spirits that were in the sacred

114

wells, on hill-tops and in groves, beneath the stones and in the hollows of the earth, gave an answer to the emptiness within.

The gentry, educated, affluent – though not necessarily wealthy – the majority well content with the new order of things, shrugged a tolerant shoulder at the superstition rife in the countryside. It did no harm. Sometimes it did good. The cowman's wife was closer to Nature than the squire's lady, and if the former had an ailing child, and doctor and physic failed to cure it, then the nurse could call at the cottage bringing an older remedy. A certain cure for whooping cough was to pass the child under the belly of a piebald horse, which animal, being rare enough, might live in a district several miles away. Its owner, however, knew its value. The mere possession of such a horse conferred status. It could be led from village to village, much as a stallion was at serving-time, while anxious mothers ran to their cottage gate with whooping babies crying in their arms.

Smallpox and measles had a different antidote. A live fowl would be taken to the patient's bedroom and hung upside-down from a beam, its feathers plucked. Within twenty-four hours the dreaded smallpox spots or the measles rash would leave the human sufferer and transfer to the still-living fowl. In a short space of time the bird turned black and congested, and with a final struggle died, while the patient, his fever gone, was free of infection. This remedy was in use up to our own times.

Many a lad, whether from manor house or cottage, could be cured of his hernia by crawling through an ash sapling before sunrise, fasting; many an infant, his palate white with thrush, has had his mouth blown into and so freed by one who never knew his own father – in other words, was born posthumously.

The cures for warts were, are even today, many and various. The persons able to effect a cure were known as "charmers," and the secret of the charm was often handed down from one generation of a family to another. Those that are repeated and passed by word of mouth would appear to have no value; thus the gathering of nine bramble leaves, and the placing of them in spring water, afterwards passing them over the diseased part, or the rubbing of a piece of meat-flesh upon the wart, then burying the flesh and letting it decay, during which time the wart disappears, must for the very broadcasting of the charm lose potency. I cured myself once of a wart upon a finger, having heard of a charm that sounded more aesthetically pleasing than anointing it with wet bramble leaves or decaying meat. The wart, which had been with me a number of years and was caused by pencil pressure when writing, vanished within a month.

If charmers were also in demand through the length and breadth of Cornwall, putting the local doctor out of business, and possibly the parson too, witches were not so popular, and were mostly dealt with in rough and ready fashion. Witchcraft, like charming, was thought to be hereditary, and those believed to have the power were looked upon by their neighbours with mistrust. It was best, when meeting them on the highway, to pass them by on the right-hand side of the road, and if by mischance one caught their eye dread consequences might befall the innocent. To be "ill-wished" was something to be avoided at all costs. Months of illness might follow, cattle fall sick, fish refuse to bite, plants wither, and the surest remedy against such disasters was to draw blood from the witch herself. Then her power ceased.

If an ox, or any other animal, died in consequence of an ill-wish it was customary to take out the creature's heart, stick it with nails and pins, and roast it before the fire until the pins dropped out one by one. The witch was supposed to suffer in sympathy with the roasting heart and was then forced to confess what she had done, and so release the animal's owner from her spell. Many Cornish villagers employed conjurers or diviners who, like witch-doctors in Africa, discovered a witch's identity by secret means. As in the jungle, old grudges against others could then be paid.

"Beware, look about you, my neighbours. If any of you have a sheep sick of the giddies, or a hog of the mumps, or a horse of the staggers, or a knavish boy of the school, or an idle girl of the wheel, or a young drab of the sullens, and hath not fat enough for her porridge, or butter enough for her bread, and she hath a little help of the epilepsy or cramp to teach her to roll her eyes, wry her neck,

116

Death waited also on the ebb of the tide.

gnash her teeth, startle with her body; hold her arms and hands stiff. And then, when an old Mother Nobbs hath by chance called her 'idle young housewife,' or bid the devil scratch her; then no doubt but old Mother Nobbs is the witch, and the young girl is owl-blasted."

Owls were always birds of ill-omen. So were ravens, croaking over a house, or a crowing hen. Pillows stuffed with the feathers of wild birds made dying painful and prolonged. Death waited also on the ebb of the tide. The appearance of a toad on the doorstep was a certain sign that the house had been ill-wished, and the toad was then put to a particularly barbarous death. Down to the present day an unwanted dog or cat, if sick or mischievous, does not invariably receive the ministration of the local vet. It is "put to cliff," that is to say tied in a bag, living, and thrown out to sea. (A sheep or bullock, straying too near to a precipitous drop and disappearing, is also said to have "gone to cliff," together with other waste matter, refuse, old bedding, broken grates.)

Lunatics, in older days, fared little better than sick animals or witches, for the treatment was to "bowssen" them in pools. The most famous pool lay below St. Nunne's Well at Altarnun, now, alas, dried up, and nothing left of it but muddied pasture, the stream having been diverted a few years since. Carew gave a full account of it in his *Survey of Cornwall* which is worth the quoting. "The water running from St. Nunne's Well fell into a square and close-walled plot, which might be filled at what depth they listed. Upon this wall was the franticke person set to stand, his backe towards the poole; and from thence, with a sudden blow in the brest, tumbled headlong into the pond, where a strong fellow, provided for the nonce, tooke him and tossed him and tossed him, up and downe, alongst and athwart the water, until the patient, by forgoing his strength, had somewhat forgot his fury. Then was he conveyed to the church, and certaine masses sung over him; upon which handling, if his right wits returned, St. Nunne had the thanks; but if there appeared small amendment, he was bowssened againe, and againe, while there remayned in him any hope of life for recovery."

Persons injured before death, whether physically or by a neighbour's spite, were never thought to rest in peace, but took the form of a white hare with burning eyes, from which dogs and beasts ran away howling. The hare indeed was the most hated of all four-footed beasts, both in west and in east Cornwall, for if it did not contain the spirit of a dead woman or a man then it was the metamorphosis of the nearest suspected witch, especially if she happened to be old, ugly, cross-tempered or, more important, lame. There was a hare in one parish that was said to have more than ordinary qualities. It defied pursuit and baffled hounds. Then one day, chased by a crowd of sportsmen, it was seen to disappear round the side of a hill, and when the pursuers caught up with it, and climbed the shielding rocks, they found no hare at all but an old, ugly woman, panting after a hard chase, with one foot lame. An ox's heart was roasted afterwards to see if the woman bled.

The hare, and later the rabbit, were held in such abhorrence by fishermen that to mention either when at sea brought spoliation of lines and nets, or dearth of fish. I learnt this to my cost at the age of twenty-one, when trying for pollack off Lantic Bay near Fowey. The weather was dull, and glancing at the cliffs near by I observed to my companion, the Cornish boatman who shared such expeditions with me, that we might have done better to stay ashore and go rabbiting instead. To my surprise he pursed his lips and slowly pulled in both our lines.

"That's done it," he said, "we'll catch no fish today." Shaking a mournful head he pulled for home. I had spoken the fatal word.

Such superstitions, which no reasoning can dispel, survive therefore to the present time, along with bonfires on Midsummer Eve and "calling the neck" at harvest – when the last stalks of the wheat-crop are gathered into a sheaf and borne home by a triumphant harvester crying, "I have him, I have him, I have him," to which his companions shout, "What have 'e?" and he replies, "A neck, a neck, a neck," whereupon the sheaf is carried to the farm kitchen and hung from a beam till the following year. Hurling still takes place on

Shrove Tuesday at St. Columb between the people of the town and those of the country, with a silver ball thrown into the air and fought for through the streets and out on the highways. At the "Furry" dancing on May 8 at Helston the local populace take to their feet and dance in and out of one another's houses, and the baiting of the hobby-horse at Padstow on May morning is a pagan pastime if ever there was one. A man, bedecked in a black tarpaulin forming a bell-like tent, a snapping mask upon his face and a painted hat upon his head, rushes at the gaping crowd about him, belaboured meanwhile by his disguised attendants. Here is something more ancient than the Biblical scapegoat: winter is being driven from our midst with all its ills. These innocent amusements gave relief through countless centuries, while the darker customs often remained unspoken and unsung.

The religious Cornishman needed an outlet for his emotions. He did not find it in the Established church. Vicars of parishes were too often relatives of the local landowner or squire, associated in the people's minds with the gentry. Church services were tedious, sermons repetitive and dull, and the people, living on a frugal diet in crowded cottages, found little to do on the drawn-out Sabbath day.

So when John Wesley travelled west in 1743 he hit Cornwall like a tornado, upsetting values, scattering the supposedly faithful, shocking parsons, disturbing landowners, shaking the bewildered people into a lively sense not only of their own shortcomings but also of their worth, should they repent of their sins, to an ever-present and a living God. Angry at first, then curious, then avid for his teaching, they flocked to listen to this thundering preacher with a fiery message, yet so small that he had to stand upon a rock to make himself heard. Here was a man who knew no distinction of persons, who reached out for the soul of fisherman or miner with total disregard for status, who called upon them in their homes, who blessed the children, and, more exciting and more devastating still, brought back to their dulling hearts all the terrors of hell fire. Repent . . . repent . . . the lake of brimstone awaited those who would not hear the word of God, eternal torment, the horrors of the damned, but for the men, women and children who put away sin, confessed their iniquities, there would be mercy, forgiveness and the everlasting arms.

This was what the Cornish people needed. Here was the outlet they desired – tears, lamentations, beatings of the breast, a falling upon the knees, the relief of confession, followed by the joys of salvation and a bursting into song. The great Revival had begun.

Wesley's triumph, bringing wave after wave of converts through succeeding years, was not without opposition. The clergy thought him a meddler, as did many of the gentry, and rumour, spreading faster in Cornwall than anywhere else in England, had it that the preacher was a supporter of Charles Edward Stuart, the Young Pretender, even that the claimant to the Hanoverian throne had disguised himself to follow in Wesley's train and was lurking in the county under an assumed name.

Tinners, spoiling for a fight of any sort, would gather outside the houses where Wesley was due to preach and endeavour to shout him

John Wesley.

down – not from hostility, but for sport. They were, in fact, among the first to succumb to his compelling words, the first to fall upon their knees.

"It is remarkable," wrote the preacher in his journal, "that those of St. Just were the chief of the whole country for hurling, fighting, drinking and all manner of wickedness; but many of the lions are become lambs, are continually praising God, and calling their old companions in sin to come and magnify the Lord together."

Wesley continued to visit Cornwall during the next forty years, and, despite occasional riots, setbacks and animosity from a minority, by the time of his last appearance there, as an old man of eighty-six in 1789, he might well have felt that he had achieved a veritable revolution. Not only had he won the hearts of the people by his magnetism, but his message had stuck. He had largely conquered the apathy, despair and general lawlessness he had found amongst so many; he had given them new hope, new faith for the future. Just as the tinners in old days had seen themselves as a race apart and somehow different from their fellow-men, so the Methodists combined in a united fellowship, recruited almost entirely from the less wealthy members of the social order. There was a re-birth of pride in work, dignity in living, tranquillity and understanding in the home. The scourge of drunkenness declined, wrecking became a thing of the past, and, although the worst of the mining misfortunes were yet to come, at the end of the eighteenth and nineteenth centuries, it was largely owing to Wesley's preaching, Wesley's teaching of love, forbearance and obedience to the word of God, that those he won, and their descendants, faced the struggle with so much fortitude.

The chapels that the Methodists built are spread over the whole of Cornwall. There is one in every village, every town. Many are simple, plain, features of the rugged landscape that begot them. Others, of a later date, are less endearing, conforming to a Victorian pattern that lacked taste. Even these, however, are typical of a people who desired their own form of worship in their own meeting-houses, submitting to no dictation, no authority from a governing class.

The most famous of the early preaching-places is Gwennap.

The most famous of the early preaching-places is Gwennap Pit, near Redruth, site of a disused mine-working, where John Wesley converted thousands in the open air. There has been a Methodist service there every Whit Monday since his death. Gwennap was also the home of Cornwall's native evangelist, the miner Billy Bray, beloved by all his comrades, who thought nothing of working underground all week and then walking more than twenty miles on Sunday to preach at a distant village. Men such as these – and he had many followers – were the true enthusiasts, living the Gospel in their daily lives, preaching and practising Christianity with all the fervour of the early Cornish saints.

Inevitably, as the years passed, the deep emotion and intrinsic simplicity of the great Revival underwent change. More prosperous members of the community became devotees, merchants, traders, councillors. Methodism had turned respectable. What had started as a spontaneous and truly emotional response of the ordinary working man developed into something less dynamic, and the first fresh impact lost its pristine quality. Hell fire was still in evidence, neighbourly love less so. Faces that had been a-glow with zeal turned

sour with disapproval. "Thou must" gave way to "Thou must not." Sunday was not so much a day of rest as a day of doom. No work, naturally – but no play either. No courting in the lanes. No fishing on the quiet. No wrestling behind the hills. No reading of any book but the Bible. Too many pursed lips, and eyes askance at young women who liked to wear a piece of finery or a saucy hat.

During the present century, as in the rest of the country, two world wars and a rise in the standard of living, along with the growth of the tourist industry, have turned Sunday into a holiday for all. Attendance at chapel is not what it was, admittedly, but men, women, children get out and about the countryside without fearing the brimstone lake. The change from a narrow viewpoint to an appreciation of a wider world is a happy result, providing the Cornishman does not lose his individuality. This must be his saving grace, and that core of emotion, wrapped in superstition, forever lurking in his soul. There are still bonfires to be lighted on Midsummer Eve, still wells beneath the tangled briars awaiting votive offerings. Warts rise on the skin that must be charmed, voices call from the sea that must be appeased, and a walk in winter on the hills may yet produce a startled hare, who, before it limps to cover, will stare back with burning eyes.

Opposite: *Voices call from the sea that must be appeased.*

Chapter Ten

ECCENTRICS

THE spirit of independence that was always so strong a feature of Cornish character was apt to turn, when nurtured in isolation, to eccentricity. Eccentrics, indeed, have abounded in the peninsula from the earliest times, the first saints being among the most spectacular, especially in the manner of their arrival from Ireland. St. Piran was said to have appeared on the beach at Perranzabuloe on a millstone, having been tied to it by pagans in his own country and thrown over a cliff, while St. Ia, founder saint of St. Ives and the daughter of an Irish chieftain, floated calmly into Hayle estuary on a leaf. St. Petroc, son of a Welsh king, landed in a more orthodox manner in the river Camel with sixty followers, but his first action was to strike water out of a rock like Moses, and he lived a life of great austerity near to Padstow before travelling to the East, where it was said that he existed for seven years on a single fish. St. Gennys was a martyr who had the unusual skill of being able to carry his head in his hands after decapitation, and St. Keyne, coming into Cornwall from Somersetshire in the seventh century, was renowned for turning adders into stones. "This woman," recorded the historian Hals, "is much wanted in Cornwall now, where adders and serpents abound to the great hurt of man and beast."

The names of places often became confused with the names of saints and pilgrims; thus the parish of Roche, dominated by a great natural rock formation in its midst from which it supposedly drew its name, was also said to have been founded by the saint Roche, born at Montpelier in France, who cured several people of the plague and then, catching it himself, withdrew to a wood so that he might not

A hermit who had his solitary cell upon a rock.

infect his neighbours, living by the kindness of a dog which every day brought him a loaf of bread. He in his turn became confused with another hermit who had his solitary cell upon the rock, being "diseased with a grievous leprosy" and ministered to by his daughter Gunett or Gundred, who fetched him water from a well near by.

St. Nectan was another hermit, who gave his name to the waterfall and glen lying a few miles inland from Tintagel. Here, above the cascading water which tumbles some forty feet or more into the basin below before coursing through the woodland in a winding stream and plunging into the deep gorge called the Rocky Valley, the hermit was said to have had his home, and supposedly lies buried under the flat stones of the basin or "Kieve" upon which the water falls. The road from Boscastle to Tintagel cuts the valley, bridging the stream, and today, in summer, with Tintagel a high spot for tourist traffic

The Rocky Valley . . . superbly dissociated from humankind.

rivalling Land's End in popularity, the hermit would find his solitude disturbed. Not so in winter. Both Rocky Valley and St. Nectan's glen have all the loneliness that the most passionate of pilgrims could desire.

The first, despite its name suggesting a tortuous climb, has a path that winds with comparative ease towards the sea, and can be followed without strain on heart or limb; yet the steepness of descent, the rugged nature of the cliffs on either side towering above the head, the dark and slippery surface of the rocks themselves, still spell disaster to the more venturesome who crane forward and downward to glimpse the rushing stream. The narrowness of the gorge impels the water, swollen with winter rains, to course the faster, and white with foam it twists and tumbles over its stony bed to a sudden flat surface where, smooth for an instant, it plunges from the canyon to the open sea. There is no cove here to receive the fall, no spit of shore, no shingle bay as at Marsland Mouth. The full surge of the Atlantic sweeps against the cliffs, forever turbulent, forever grey, like the rocks encompassing the gully, awaiting at flood tide or at ebb the torrent from the Rocky Valley.

If this was where the hermit walked in centuries gone by, then nothing has changed. The ceaseless sound of water is the same, the tumble of foam into the sea, the slippery surface of the rocks that winter or summer will never dry. The place has the impersonality of somewhere superbly dissociated from humankind, even from life itself. There are no gulls perching upon the ledges or the clefts, no sheep grazing on the headlands beyond. The force of matter is pre-eminent, hard rock challenging the elemental thrust of water. Perhaps this was what drew the hermit to wander here from his cell higher up the valley, endeavouring to reconcile the indifference of nature with an all-seeing and benevolent God.

There is no outlet seaward for the wanderer, who must retrace his steps and climb back to the road, then, crossing it, strike upwards through the wooded valley in search of St. Nectan's waterfall.

The scene changes, the rugged grandeur disappears. The close-packed trees drip melancholy, growing ever thicker and more dense, and the winding stream patters its way through undergrowth and seeping moss. The air, even in winter, is oppressive, heavy with damp. Stepping-stones ford the stream at intervals, but these, after a wet winter, become dislodged and carried away, and there is no remedy but to leap the stream itself, if the walker has agility, or cling desperately to an overhanging branch of some dead tree, and swing awhile, like Absalom, before risking the final lunge to the opposite bank. Rotting trunks are everywhere, fungus-filled and reeking to the touch, and what path there is, or was, is overlaid with briars, yet leads incessantly upward through the glen, towards the sound of the distant waterfall. Despair sets in. The wanderer will not make it, and realizes with a pounding heart that the time is already five past four and darkness is not far away, earlier here in the woods than in the open. Besides, what if the rotten branch that serves as handrail breaks on the backward trail, and a horrid plunge, waist-deep into turgid water, is the result?

But, as Childe Roland to the Dark Tower came, he must go on, nought else remains to do. St. Nectan turns to myth, but his cell at least might be a resting-place. Or something less welcoming, perhaps. For the walker remembers another, and later, legend connected with the valley, dating back no more than a century and a half, which has all the exaggeration yet authenticity of Cornish gossip in its heyday.

There were two women once, so the story ran, who came to St. Nectan's cell when it was still a place of habitation – a cottage, that is to say, built on the site where the hermit lived. The inhabitants of Bossiney, the nearest village, knew nothing of these women, neither their history nor where they had come from. They never even learnt their names. They were supposedly of gentle birth, for their manners were grave and dignified, and they paid for every purchase made, but they encouraged no questions, nor did they ask any themselves, but remained quietly aloof, month after month, in their cottage by the waterfall. They had no servant and received no visitor, and it was noticed that when they went to the village, or walked in the valley, one was never seen without the other. Suspicion grew. It was said, amongst the villagers, that the pair spoke to one another in an unknown language, whispering very low, as if fearful of being heard, and that this language was surely of devil's origin, that the two communed with spirits when they were alone. No villager, however, was ill-wished. None of them could prove a spell. Not even a wild cat crossed the cottage threshold that might have been assumed to act as a familiar. Whatever the ladies did, they did alone.

At last rumour had it that one of them was dead, and, curiosity being too much to stifle, the nearest neighbours walked up the valley to see if this was true. Rumour, for once, had not lied. The neighbours penetrated the cottage, and found one of the two ladies weeping beside the bedside of her friend. The friend was dead. How long she had been ill, how long she had lain dead, no one could discover. The survivor gave no information, answered no questions, she did not even look up when the questioners begged her, for her own sake, to tell them what she knew, or at least to give them some instruction as to burial. Nothing but silence, and the quiet weeping. Finally it was arranged between the neighbours that the corpse must be taken up and removed from the cottage, and then interred with the usual Christian rites. This action on their part would surely stir the weeping one from her chair beside the bed. It had no effect. She let them take the body of her friend away. It was growing dark and no one wished to stay, so they left the survivor in her chair, thinking that perhaps the morning would bring her to her senses and that she would descend to the village, either for information or for food.

Days, passed, but still she did not leave the cottage. People waited in the valley thinking she might come. They crept to the window and looked in, but she had not moved. Perhaps, they thought, she had no need for food, but was ministered to in some mysterious fashion by powers from the nether regions, and, if disturbed, calamity might fall upon them all.

One morning a child, who was bolder than her elders, looked in at the window and saw that the lady sat even more motionless than usual, with her hand hanging stiffly from her chair, the handkerchief she always held lying upon the floor. The child ran home and reported what she had seen. Once again the neighbours climbed the valley to the cottage and went inside. They found the survivor of the two friends stiff and cold in her chair, her eyes wide open, her body worn by starvation to a skeleton frame. They took her and buried her as they had buried her friend, no one knowing, then or later, the true history of the ladies of St. Nectan's glen.

Hardly a tale for a wet walk in winter, when a twisted ankle might bring the wayfarer to a desperate plight, with only the trees for cover. Already the waterfall sounds loud and clear, deafening thought, and by dint of climbing, slipping, death in every step, the torrent is perceived, cold and impersonal as the other fall in the Rocky Valley; but while the latter tumbled in fierce haste to join the sea this water has a more majestic flow, white as a deistic beard, splashing with imperturbability into St. Nectan's Kieve below.

A voice from the jutting rocks above calls out, "No photographs without permission!" The saint in person? Has apprehension done its worst and conjured forth his spirit? An answer brings reassurance, and with it anti-climax. St. Nectan's cell, or rather its foundation, is now the home, not of two lonely ladies, but of a bright-eyed married couple from Weston-super-Mare, who have bought and redecorated the decaying cottage and show the falls to visitors in the summer season. Tea is proffered and gratefully received, and compliments exchanged. The husband disappears to paint the kitchen, his wife informs the wanderer that she is psychic. Knocking is heard at midnight. Footsteps echo when the moon is full. So the tale of the two fond friends is really true? Yes, but a different version, more suited, it would seem, to those tourists who express a wish to see the water flow into St. Nectan's Kieve. The ladies were St. Nectan's sisters and looked after him. All three lie buried in the basin beneath the fall. No, the bones have never been found; nevertheless they are said to repose beneath the slabs of stone.

The wanderer, disenchanted, prefers the version known to Wilkie Collins when he climbed the glen in 1850, and to Mr. White of London who did the same in 1854. The tale, as told to them, was no more than half a century old. The ladies had no connection then with the mythical saint. They were eccentrics, seeking solitude for no better reason than that they liked it.

There is further disappointment still to come. No need to retrace faltering footsteps through the valley. No necessity, even, to have climbed the wooded glen up to the falls. A path from the cottage leads across fields and over a stile to the main road. It takes five minutes. The two eccentrics must have walked this way to Bossiney when they made their weekly purchases, and possibly never wandered in the valley after all. Disillusion is complete, though faith in eccentricity remains.

There is no doubt about the identity of Daniel Gumb, a stone-cutter by trade, born in the parish of Lezant in the Hundred of East Wivel, close to the eastern fringe of the Bodmin moors. He had a passion for mathematics and astronomy, and, breaking loose from his fellow-men and the conventions of ordinary life, took up a new existence on a spot not far from the great formation called the Cheesewring. Here he hollowed out a crevice in the rocks, widening a recess already there, which, with a slab above it, formed a natural cave. It was big enough to take him and his wife and children, if they rolled themselves sideways to enter into it. He never left it, nor did they, while they lived.

Persons who wish to live separately from their fellows, or die differently, tend to build follies, and one such was Sir James Tillie, who lived at Pentillie castle on the banks of the Tamar, near the parish of St. Mellion. He built himself a tower called Mount Ararat, north of the castle, and left instructions in his will, when he died in 1712, that this must be his place of burial. His body was to be fastened to his chair with iron, and he was to be dressed in his best clothes, his wig and hat upon his head, and near him an oak chest with all his books and papers, for within two years he would rise again and return to Pentillie castle. The instructions were carried out, but alas for prophecy! within two years Sir James's body was eaten up by worms, his skeleton had fallen from the chair, and wig and clothes were likewise rotted. His remains are in the tower today, unfortunately not visible, but in a coffin.

The Rev. Hawker of Morwenstow in Stratton, who became famous for his attempts to save the lives of shipwrecked sailors, many of whom lie buried in his churchyard, a figurehead marking their graves, cannot in all fairness be called an eccentric: other vicars nearer to our own time deserve the name more richly. A parson, when he turns odd, does it thoroughly, especially if he lives in Cornwall; in fact, he may be said to go the whole hog. Whether it is that the climate gets into his bones, or that until quite recently the Methodists stole away his flock, thus giving him more time to commune alone with the Almighty, is hard to say. Isolation does strange things to the religiously trained.

Some years ago there was a vicar with a parish bordering the river Fal whose whim it was to sleep by day and visit his parishioners by night. This proved disconcerting to those who, fast asleep, awoke startled to the peal of a bell or loud knocking upon the door, and fearing thieves descended the stairs to find a bland and smiling parson calling for an hour's chat and a cup of tea. The vicar was unmarried and lived with his sister, who would go with him on his nightly prowls, but his great solace was to play the church organ from midnight onwards, and any villager who happened to be abroad by night would hear loud strains of music coming from the church. If he had the courage to peep inside he would catch a glimpse of the vicar himself, seated at the organ, letting himself go in triumphant melody, while his sister was curled up in one of the pews asleep.

This vicar at any rate was happy, and had his sister for companion, but another further north was left a widower with two small daughters, and as his rectory adjoined farm-buildings under his care it seemed to him that the wisest thing to do was to bring up the children in the barn, along with the cocks and hens, for here they could come to no harm when he was out and about on parish business, and would have the poultry for company. The idea, if sound in theory, failed in practice, for hens are poor instructors except to their own offspring, and the two small girls grew into their teens with little or no knowledge of life outside the barn. They were,

A figurehead marking their graves.

when the manner of their housing was finally discovered and other arrangements made, if not maladjusted at least ill-adapted to a world which they looked upon with bewildered eyes.

The most eccentric of Cornish vicars, not indigenous to the county, and the most lonely, was the Rev. Densham of Warleggan, who came to his parish in the 1920s. Warleggan, remote and isolated in West Wivel in the south-eastern part of Bodmin moor, had suffered ill-luck a hundred years before, in 1818, when lightning struck the church tower in a storm, shivering it to pieces. The clerk, passing through the churchyard at the time, narrowly escaped the falling stones. This omen, to the superstitious, might have suggested heavenly wrath upon the parish. If so, it took over a hundred years to strike again, and when it came, came more insidiously.

I first heard of the Rev. Densham when a friend of mine in Fowey, the same with whom I camped near Land's End, told me that a vicar, newly inducted in a moorland parish, had been brought by a fellow-clergyman to her parents' home for Sunday tea. He was amiable enough, even loquacious, although, so she thought, a little odd. "In what way?" I enquired, wondering perhaps if here was yet another who would call on his parishioners at midnight. "He asked me," she said, "to recommend a gardener to live in." He was a bachelor, and whomever he employed would receive for his services a penny a year and all his potatoes free.

"I told him," said my friend, the most courteous of persons, "that gardeners were rather hard to find, and possibly the wages he suggested were a little low."

Here, for the time being, the matter ended. The vicar returned to his parish without his gardener, nor, it seemed, did he find one locally who was willing to enter his service upon such conditions. Months passed, and my friend heard rumours from time to time that all was not well at Warleggan; the parishioners were not happy with their vicar. He had spent, so it was said, long years abroad and seemed unaccustomed to their ways. The sparseness of the congregation, never large at any time owing to its remote situation, displeased him, and he would prop up images of wood or cardboard in the pews to swell the ranks.

Despite his desire for a full church, the vicar never went into the village or visited his flock. He placed a box upon his garden gate, at the entrance to the drive, in which all such provisions as he needed had to be placed, together with his post, thus denying passage to all comers. He erected fences surmounted by barbed wire, over eight feet in height, around his entire property, so that he could live as one in a state of siege; and for greater protection he imported some half-dozen large and savage dogs, mostly Alsatians, which, at the first sound of prowling footstep in the lane beyond, leapt snarling at the fence like a pack of wolves.

The parishioners, frightened nearly out of their wits, protested to the Bishop, but as the vicar had done nothing to offend ecclesiastical law the authorities of the Church were powerless to remove him. He took the services on Sundays, although by now there was nobody present but the cardboard images, and for this strict observance he must still be assumed to be a man of God.

A moment came when he advertised for an organist, and the unsuspecting visitor, arriving after dark, was shown into the rectory by the vicar, finding it, to his surprise and dismay, almost totally unfurnished. The bedroom into which he was thrust, with the door locked upon him from the outside, had only packing-cases against the walls and sacks upon the floor. Two versions are given of the luckless organist's escape. One, that the vicar led him twice to church and conducted every service in the prayer-book, feeding him afterwards upon corned beef and half a loaf; the other that he escaped that night from his bedroom window, braving the Alsatian dogs, and made his way over the moor to Bodmin. Whichever is true, the organist departed within twelve hours, and never saw the vicar or Warleggan again.

It was after hearing this tale that my friend and I decided to make our way to Jamaica Inn on Bodmin moor, a place of refuge known to both of us from riding days, and sally forth the following day to call upon the vicar.

The trek was long, the day was hot – surprisingly, for mid-May – and Warleggan was not easy to find. We arrived weary and already rather scared, having eaten a pasty lunch unwittingly upon a nest of adders, the strange hissing noise beneath warning us, just before they uncoiled and rose, that the stone was occupied. Warleggan church already had an air of desolation, the small churchyard tall

The church already had an air of desolation.

with unkempt grass, the silence profound. No one, save the pastor, had said a prayer within for many years. Our courage waned. We left the church and approached the rectory, which was screened by tall trees nested in by colonies of rooks whose restless cawing held a baleful note.

We found the entrance gate barred and wired, with the box upon it for provisions empty. Daringly, we sounded the bell. Hardly had it clanged than eight – my companion afterwards said ten – enormous dogs, wolf-hounds and Alsatians, sprang from nowhere upon the fence above us, leaping, snarling, yellow fangs bared in rage. Like the organist, we fled in terror to the moor, preferring the nest of adders to this pack of hungry dogs, and there consulted as to our next move. Prudence overcame our love for adventure, and we decided to make the next onslaught by car, but not till a year or so later did the opportunity arise to brave Warleggan once again.

This time we were three, our chaffeur being a mutual friend and writer who, having travelled the world and crossed Alaska, had greater stamina than either of us. Unluckily, she did not care for dogs. These, at all costs, must be avoided. She parked the car, well hidden, in a nearby lane, and we skirted the rectory garden. Once again the baleful rooks arose, giving warning of our presence, but the dogs were silent. Possibly they had starved to death. The fence about the garden had a worn, almost battered appearance.

"We'll climb the hedge at the far end," whispered the explorer from Alaska. "We may find the vicar strolling in the garden."

She was right. Struggling up the bank, gaining a foothold amongst the briars and nettles, ignoring the barbed wire, we caught our breath in wonder. There was the vicar, scarcely twenty yards away, pacing up and down his little plot of ground, a strange, unbelievable figure in a dark frockcoat green with age, a black shovel hat upon his head.

We stared. He did not see us. Up and down he walked, with heaven knows what melancholy thoughts, what lonely speculations. Suddenly the explorer did a crazy thing. She took her handkerchief from her pocket and began to wave it wildly in the air.

"Cooee!" she shouted. "Cooee!"

The vicar paused. He lifted his head a moment to right and left, then stalked away, his hands behind his back. Scarlet with shame, I plucked the explorer from the hedge. The last of the trio was already running for the car. This expedition, like the first, had proved ignominious. We retreated, cowed.

These happenings were all of thirty years ago, and the three of us have reproached ourselves since for hooligan behaviour, and for having omitted to try the entrance drive, for the dogs, as we discovered afterwards, had gone. The vicar had been alone. Possibly he might have received us, possibly our visit might have done some good. For the sequel was tragic. The Rev. Densham survived many years in solitude and silence, until one day, no sign of him having been seen about his churchyard, no smoke coming from the rectory chimney, some of his parishioners ventured to the house and forced an entry. The place was littered with paper and wood shavings, floorboards had been torn up to serve as fuel for his fire, and the vicar himself lay dead upon the stairs.

Since then there has been no resident incumbent at Warleggan, and a clergyman from another parish comes to do duty on a Sunday.

Last winter, wishing to revive old memories, I told my son the story and we ventured to Warleggan for a final visit. Whether from stupidity, or my usual misreading of the map, the village was still difficult to find. Signposts pointed in the wrong direction, side-roads turned to impassable tracks, and the foreboding that we were to be benighted on the moor – a recurrent nightmare, for it has happened to me in the past – returned with all its brooding horror.

At last, with the sun setting in a watery sky, I saw the clump of trees against a nearby hill, and the outline of the church. Warleggan was before us. The church, humped and desolate within its walls, looked just as it had done some thirty years earlier, the tall grass untouched. We tried the door, but it was locked. We turned away and made for the rectory drive. Remains of the fence still straddled the wall, but there was no barricade, and the gate opened to the touch. The drive was overgrown, with tangled shrubs touching each other's heads and leaning branches forming archways high above. We rounded a corner, the driveway petering out to a narrow path, and there was the rectory I had so often thought about and longed to look upon. The walls were a melancholy green, the windows dark; the house had all the sadness of a place unvisited and in decay. I remembered the vicar pacing in the garden behind the house, in his green frockcoat, his shovel hat upon his head. We stared in silence until a cat startled us, running from the bushes, and unmistakably, below the drive, came the sound of a car. My son, undefeated, crept closer to the house to take his picture. I summoned all the aplomb of an inveterate trespasser, and walked down the drive.

There was a jeep parked just outside the gate, and from it stepped a man wearing a beret. I began a torrent of explanations, how I had known the Rev. Densham in the past, that I had often sought to call

The house had all the sadness of a place unvisited and in decay.

upon him without success, and that my son was even now taking a photograph of the rectory. The man in the beret smiled. He walked with me up the drive and said that he leased the place now, but that his wife and family did not care to live there, so he only came from time to time to see that all was well. My son emerged from the bushes, stammering apologies.

"The Rev. Densham," I said, retreating slowly, "used to walk about the place alone. I climbed a hedge and saw him once, many, many years ago."

The man looked first at me, then at my son. "He still walks," he said softly, "back there, in the garden," and motioned us forward. The light was fading fast, and the cat that we had startled from the bushes came out on to the path and mewed.

"I think," I said to my son, "we ought to be getting home," and to our friend in the beret, "We have rather far to go . . ."

He nodded, smiling, and moved towards the house. We walked to the curve in the drive and then, with one accord, ran to the entrance gate, past the jeep, and down the lane to where we had left the car. Only when we reached it did we dare to look at one another.

I glanced over my shoulder to the shadowed drive. The jeep, parked outside the rectory gate, looked like an army vehicle on patrol, and its owner, skirting the house and prowling somewhere in the grounds, suggested sentry-duty; but for what? Did he stand there during the hours of darkness, with the cat mewing at his feet, waiting for a figure to emerge in a frockcoat and shovel hat who, when challenged, stalked away, hands clasped behind his back? Had eccentricity claimed another victim, environment this time the infecting cause?

We drove away in the fading light, and as the comfortable sound of the car's engine broke the silence the rooks in the trees above us gathered and cawed in final protestation.

Chapter Eleven

MOORS AND CLAYPITS

THE whole of Cornwall's backbone, running from the source of Tamar in Stratton Hundred in the north to the descending land in the south-west where the rising Hayle divides Kerrier from Penwith, was once moor or downland, and the motorist who takes the main road today, remembering that he follows the route of pack-horse, mule and ox in centuries gone by, will notice that he is always on high ground. There are wooded valleys between the folds of hills, towns and villages are built on either side of his approach, but if the latter were swept away the land beneath them would be moorland scrub.

The backbone is, in fact, a high plateau, descending slowly as Cornwall narrows, only to rise and broaden out with Goonhilly Downs behind the Lizard peninsula, and again to the highlands of West Penwith and the Land's End claw.

The greatest and wildest stretch of moorland is the land mass south of Launceston, north of Bodmin, reaching east as far as Liskeard, and west beyond Camelford almost to Tintagel and the coast. The main road cuts across the centre from Five Lanes, and in summer a stream of cars and coaches passes along it with holiday-makers coastward bound, but in winter the road is almost as free from traffic as it was in earlier days. Rough tracks lead to isolated farms whose inhabitants once hardly ventured forth except to market, owners of sheep and cattle who lived on their own produce and cut moorland turf for fuel. The wanderer who is fond of solitude can wander anywhere on either side of the main road and lose himself forthwith, turning, after he has walked barely half a mile in open country, to see no sign of human habitation, nothing but bare

143

brown moor as far as the eye can reach, rising in the distance to frowning tors and craggy rocks that might give shelter if a rain-shower came, but little comfort from the wind which seeks out clefts and crannies even if the day is still.

Brown Willy, 1375 feet, and Rough Tor, its companion near to Camelford, are the highest hills, often climbed by straggling parties in a dry season, the view stupendous when the weather is clear, stretching to the coasts on either side and away down the peninsula past the china-clay pyramids almost as far as West Penwith. The river Fowey rises beneath Brown Willy, and originally this whole district was known as Fawey moor. The ground here is soggy, treacherous, betraying its presence by a darker green and tufts of grass, some-times with reedy stems, which to the ignorant might seem as firm as the coarser hussocks of the higher ground near by, until weight put upon them makes them sag, tremble, and sink to oozing water. Deception is all around, for the turf one has just travelled no longer appears safe but trembles too, and panic sets in with each faltering step. The secret is never to descend, if possible, to what seems smooth and easy pasture lying low, for here are the intersecting streams, the bogs, the marshes, traps not only for the walker but for straying sheep and cattle that in a wet winter are imprisoned, lost, their carcasses fed upon by the more wily fox or plucked from above by hawk and buzzard, until nothing remains but bones and skull bleached white.

The moorland east of the main road, above the Fowey stream and the Withey Brook, is even more hazardous, for the walker sets off in good heart on high and firm land, believing he has only to traverse the plateau to find himself, after five miles or so, on the wooded slopes of Trebartha and North Hill village. Instead, the woods remain a mirage only. Crags more menacing and bleak than Brown Willy and Rough Tor loom before him, barring progress, and instinct, almost invariably wrong on these occasions, directs him to walk to the right, where the ground descends, and stops him in mid-track again, for here is another stream, another marsh, and to pursue this track petering into bog can only lead to disaster. I know, for I have tried it.

144

Foolheartedly, long ago, on a November afternoon, a friend and I –
the same companion to Land's End and Warleggan – departed on
horseback from Jamaica Inn with the happy intention of calling on an
elderly lady living at Trebartha Hall near North Hill. Surely, we told
ourselves, it would be no more than forty minutes' ride at most; and
if we stayed to tea then we must make up our minds to skirt the moor
on our homeward track, and jog back to Jamaica Inn by road.
Irresponsible, we trotted off across the moor no later than two
o'clock, only to find after an hour or more that we were little nearer to
our destination, that tors and boulders inaccessible on horseback,
even perhaps on foot, barred our passage. The track leading us on
descended to a slippery path that disappeared, while beneath us a
battered gate, swinging by the hinges, gave access to a swollen
stream. The day, comparatively fine until that moment, darkened,
and a black cloud, trailing ribbons, hovered above our heads and
burst.

In a moment all was desolation. The ominous stream rushed by
with greater swiftness, turning to a torrent. Forcing the horses up a
steep incline, to put distance between ourselves and the running
water, our heads bent low to our saddles, we plunged onward,
seeking escape. A deserted cottage, humped beneath the hill,
seemed our only hope – at least it would be temporary refuge until
the cloudburst ceased. We rode towards it, dismounted, and led our
horses to the rear. The cottage was not only empty but part fallen,
with rain driving through the empty windows, and what roof there
was had been repaired with corrugated tin, so that the cascading rain
sounded like hailstones on its surface. We leant against the fungoid
walls and brooded, Trebartha Hall a hundred miles away, Jamaica Inn
an equal distance, and all the while the rain fell upon the corrugated
roof to echo in a splashing water-butt near by. I had never known
greater despondency.

It rained for a full hour, then turned to drizzle and dank fog, by
which time our world was murky and we had lost all sense of
compass points. Emerging from the ruins my companion, a better
horsewoman than I and owner of both our steeds, looked about her

and observed, "There's nothing for it but to get into the saddle, leave our reins loose on their necks, and let them lead us home."

I was not impressed by her suggestion, for where was home to the horses – thirty miles or more to Fowey, or back across the moors to Jamaica Inn? We mounted once again, darkness and silence all about us, save for that dreary patter on the cottage roof, and somewhere to our right the hissing stream.

The horses, sure-footed even amongst dead heather and loose stones, plodded forward without hesitation, and there was some relief at least to be away from the abandoned cottage and in the open, however desolate, for there had been no warmth within its walls, no memories of hearths glowing with turf fire kindled by owners in the past. Surely whoever lived there before he let it fall to ruins had been sullen and morose, plagued by the Withey Brook that ran somewhere below his door, and in despair went out one night and drowned himself. I suggested this to my fellow-traveller, who was not amused, especially as the horses seemed attracted to the river sound. Gaining higher ground we found ourselves facing a new hazard in the form of what appeared to be a disused railway track, upon which our mounts slithered and stumbled. A railroad in mid-moor. It could not be. Unless we had both gone mad and this was fantasy.

"A line for trolleys," said my companion, "leading to a stone-quarry. If the horses take us there they'll break their legs. Better dismount." Bogs, quarries, brooks, boulders, hell on every side, we led the horses from the slippery track, and then got up on our saddles once again. I remembered an illustration from a book read long ago in childhood, *Sintram, And His Companions*, where a dispirited knight had travelled such a journey with the devil in disguise, who called himself The Little Master. It showed a terrified steed rearing near a precipice. This was to be our fate, and The Little Master would come and claim us.

The horses, bolder now they were free of the trolley-lines, headed steadily forward, straight across the moor, possibly in the direction of those menacing crags that we had seen in early afternoon, pointing

146

Jamaica Inn.

dark fingers to the sky, which, we knew very well, lay contrary to any path for home.

It was seven, it was nine, it was midnight – too dark to see our watches, and fumbling fingers could not strike damp matches. On, forever on, nothing on all sides but waste and moor.

Suddenly my companion cried, "They've done it . . . they've done it . . . Isn't that the road?"

Peering into the darkness ahead I saw a break in the rising ground, and a new flatness, and there, not a hundred yards distant, the blessed streaky wetness of the Launceston–Bodmin road, and surprisingly, unbelievably, the gaunt chimneys of Jamaica Inn itself.

"I told you so," called the expert, "horses always know the way. They travel by instinct. See, the people from the Inn have come to look for us," and sure enough there were figures with tossing lanterns wandering to and fro upon the road, and welcoming lamplight shone from the slated porch. In an instant fear was forgotten, danger had never been. It was just eight o'clock, the landlord and his wife had only then begun to think of us, and here was the turf fire for which we had longed, brown and smoky sweet, a supper of eggs and bacon ready to be served with a pot of scalding tea.

Today all is changed, and, as the poet Yeats once said, "changed utterly." Motor-coaches, cars, electric light, a bar, dinner of river-trout, baths for the travel-stained instead of a cream-jug of hot water. As a motorist I pass by with some embarrassment, feeling myself to blame, for out of that November evening long ago came a novel which proved popular, passing, as fiction does, into the folk-lore of the district. As the author I am flattered, but as a one-time wanderer dismayed.

Trebartha Hall, where we had hoped to call that afternoon, was pulled down some years ago, while the craggy hills that seemed to bar our progress, Trewortha Tor, Hawk's Tor, Kilmar Tor, frown down upon the landscape with less malevolence when approached from the east, and are easily reached by a steep car-climb from North Hill village and then a brief trek on foot. The approach from the front that we tried still appears hazardous, but hardly stuff for nightmare, unless we had indeed ventured to traverse the dreaded Withey Brook and the formidable marsh to which it leads. As for the trolley-track, diligent search has revealed no trace of it – the quarries were much further south, and out of our range. Whether we were nearer to Jamaica Inn than we imagined, or further away, is something I shall never discover; all I know is that beyond Withey Brook, between the largest tors, lies the romantic-sounding Twelve Men's Moor, teeming with granite boulders and broken stones, plashed about with seeping bogs. If this was where we rode in darkness, my salutation is overdue to the dozen men who in 1284 held it on lease from Henry, Prior of Launceston. The land was granted to them at a rent of four silver shillings a year, to be paid at Michaelmas, in return for homage and service, and the twelve men had their farms spaced out with the right of pasture over it.

Thomas and David of Kelnystok, William Foth, Robert Faber, Jordan Cada, Robert Broda, Walter la Lak, Robert Le Legha, Roger Boglawoda, John Can, William of Trewortha, Nicholas Cada – here are names for the etymologist; perhaps Walter la Lak had his farm bordering a stream, and beneath that now abandoned cottage with the corrugated roof would be thirteenth-century foundations. Life was never easy for the moorland farmer, though wool in earlier days might have fetched a price, had he stock enough to make it worth his while. But summer as well as winter would take toll of his beasts, and he needed greater courage and staying power than the farmer in the valley.

When the Twelve Men lived upon their moor there was, a few miles to the west of them, a chapel known in Edward I's day as the Capella de Temple. This was the property of the Knights Templars of Jerusalem, who by nature of their fraternity assisted all pilgrims and strangers who wished to visit the Sepulchre in the Holy Land. The chapel was built for the repose of such pilgrims, for worship and for contemplation, and was exempt from the Bishop's jurisdiction. The vicar or curate at Temple could marry without banns or licence anyone who applied to him, and, since the chapel was near to the only road across the moors between Launceston and Bodmin, this made it handy for those who wished to take advantage of its privileges. "Lying in a wild wastrell, exempted from the Bishop's Jurisdiction, many a bad marriage-bargain is there yearly slubbered up; and grass widows with their fatlings put to lie and nurse here," wrote the chronicler Tonkin.

Between Temple and Twelve Men's Moor the wayfarer in the past (or the motorist today, for a road skirts close to it) found himself surprised by an inland lake, a mile in circumference, lying in a flat hollow between the hills. This is Dozmare Pool, a sheet of water that people in old days believed bottomless; and because of it legend grew that this was where Bedivere threw the sword Excalibur, seized in mid-lake by a thrice-waving hand which fastened upon the hilt and then withdrew to unplumbed depths. Pagan myth, older than the Arthur story, said that a giant chieftain who bade his daughters slay their husbands on their marriage-night had his hunting-grounds near by, but the gods, displeased with his command, doomed him for evermore to empty the waters of the pool with a limpet-shell. In time tradition placed this punishment upon a real personage, John Tregeagle, steward to Lord Robartes of Lanhydrock in the seventeenth century, hated by all the tenants, and so the stories spread and grew, became confused, turning the pool for all time to a place of uneasy memories.

Dozmare has many moods. It is still and limpid on a summer's day, tempting to the paddler, but once a whisper of a breeze ripples the surface the colour changes to a slaty grey, ominous and drear, and little wavelets splash the shore, pebbled with brown stones and peaty mud. Then we forget that it is only five feet deep, and look for the rising hand to break the surface, reaching for Excalibur, or listen for the thin note of a demon's hunting-horn, calling hounds to the chase, pursuing the chieftain giant, so the legend runs, some sixteen miles westward across the moors to Roche.

It was on this high plateau, encompassing White Moor and Hensbarrow Downs, eastward to Luxulyan and St. Austell, west to Goss Moor and Indian Queens, that one William Cookworthy, a Plymouth Quaker, founded the china-clay industry, absorbing into it many tin-workers in the district who through lack of work found themselves in distress. Today the industry is the greatest in all Cornwall, and on July 26, 1966, received the Queen's Award.

"China clay," so Mr. Black's nineteenth-century Guide informed its readers, "is a species of moist granite – that is, the rock once so firm and tenacious has been reduced by decomposition into a soft adhesive substance, not unlike mortar, and this, when purified from mica, schorl, or quartz, is admirably adapted for the manufacture of the best kinds of pottery. It is identical with Chinese kaolin, or porcelain clay. This is piled in stopes or layers, upon an inclined plane, and a stream of water is then directed over it, which carries

Dozmare has many moods.

with it the finer and purer portions, and deposits them in a large reservoir, while the coarser residuum is caught in pits placed at suitable intervals. From the reservoir all the water is drawn off, and the clay removed to pans, where it is passed under the influence of a novel drying-machine, thoroughly relieved of moisture, properly packed up in barrels, and removed to the seaside for shipment.''

The process is more elaborate now. Mechanical excavators, hydraulic pumps, separators, refiners, all are employed in the various stages of turning kaolinized granite into solid clay, used for many purposes besides pottery, while the industrial area, roughly some twenty-five miles in circumference, is a world on its own, as sharply individual as the tin and copper districts in former centuries. Bugle, Stenalees, Foxhole, Nanpean, Treviscoe, St. Stephen's-in-Brannel, St. Dennis, these were villages or scattered hamlets once, and have developed solely on account of china-clay, housing the majority of its workers.

The men are specialists, brought up to clay from birth, second and third generation, and, like the tinners before them, have the same sense of solidarity. Clay derives from rock, from granite, just as tin does, and no matter what methods are used today, what mechanical or electric power, these men have in their blood and bones the spirit of the old tinners who struck and pounded granite long before them. It is their clay, their industry; disputes between management and men are few, almost negligible, the associated companies known as English China Clays giving a splendid example to other industrial teams.

The interest to the layman, though, and to the casual wanderer who finds himself by chance or intention in the china-clay country, is the strange, almost fantastic beauty of the landscape, where spoil-heaps of waste matter shaped like pyramids point to the sky, great quarries formed about their base descending into pits filled with water, icy green like arctic pools. The pyramids are generally highest, and the pools deepest, on land which is no longer used; the spoil-heaps sprout grass-seed, even gorse, upon the pumice-stone quality of their surface, and the water in the pits, deeper far than

Dozmare, is there because the clay has been sucked off and work begun again on virgin ground.

These clay-heaps, with their attendant lakes and disused quarries, have the same grandeur as tin mines in decay but in a wilder and more magical sense, for they are not sentinels of stone or brick constructed to house engines but mountains formed out of the rocky soil itself, and the pools, man-made, are augmented by water seeping from underground sources and by the winter rains. Sites in full production may work close at hand, cranes swing wide, trolley-buckets climb to the summit of a waste-heap, looking at a distance as small as a child's toy, before unloading and returning to base, lorries pass in and out of entrances to the road, the precincts barred by wire and DANGER notices; but the discarded pyramids and pools seem as remote from the industry near by as any lonely tor upon the moors.

Wild flowers straggle across the waste, seeds flourish into name-less plants, wandering birds from the moorland skim the lakes or dabble at the water's edge. Seagulls, flying inland, hover above the surface. There is nothing ugly here. Cornishmen are wresting a living from the granite as they have done through countless generations, leaving nature to deal in her own fashion with forgotten ground, which, being prodigal of hand, she has done with a lavish and a careless grace.

The highest point in this lunar landscape is the 1027-foot beacon on Hensbarrow Downs, from where the whole fantastic conical chain can be seen spreading west towards St. Dennis and Nanpean, or splayed out fanwise to north and south in indiscriminate heaps. Beside the beacon are ancient barrows, communal burial-places of those who settled here in prehistoric times, and the beacon itself was once the site of a watchhouse, like others on high points, where a man would lodge himself to watch for the approach of enemies on sea or land, and, if he sighted them, kindle a fire to warn his fellows.

A stranger set down upon this spot today, or closer still amongst the slag and shale, white hills on either side of him, would think himself a thousand miles from Cornwall, in the canyons of Colorado, perhaps, or the volcanic craters on the moon. Sense of orientation goes awry, as it does on Bodmin moor, and although roads intersect the vast expanse, and signposts give direction, some strange instinct compels the unwary motorist or walker to travel in a circle, the waste-heaps and pitted pools becoming all alike, and there seems no way out, no means of escape from this fantastic world. Streams run from the watershed milky white, but one of them may lead only to another pool, and the search must begin again to find a road that has no DANGER board nailed upon strings of wire. Finally a lorry, loaded with lumps of clay and speeding east, solves the perplexity. No other answer but to follow blindly in its wake, no matter where it goes, and providentially a descent begins, not to a pit but past scattered cottages heralding life, until, twisting, turning, the road emerges on to familiar ground, the grey roofs of St. Austell town no more than a couple of miles or so away.

The clayman, like the tinner, is an individual with his own traditions, but an industry rapidly becoming mechanised and ex-

The clayman, like the tinner, is an individual with his own traditions.

This strange white world of pyramid and pool.

panding all the time is, alas, unlikely to produce myth or legend. No knackers beckon from the pyramids, no water-sprite lurks in the deep pools. Or, if they do, the layman has not yet heard tell of them. Isolation, the breeding-ground of fear and mystery, is no more.

Whether china-clay will be found in greater quantities elsewhere in the world, so that the bottom drops out of the Cornish market as it did with tin a century ago, is always possible – this is a gamble "diggers" have to take. The consequences would be disastrous for the clay-worker, just as it was for his forebears who mined for tin. The land from Bugle to Indian Queens, white and pitted and scarred, its lofty pinnacles left desolate, would hardly be fitted for some new and different venture, for, as the *Parochial History of St. Dennis* says, "It is upon a bleak elevation, surrounded with a direful strag of rocks, visible above ground, of various and tremendous shapes and sizes, affording shelter and pasture for little else besides sheep,

155

rabbits, hares, goats and horses." What is more, "Upon these stones, in the year 1664 at night, rained for about an acre of ground of them, a shower of blood, which fell down in drops of the breadth of a shilling sterling, which blood remained visible on these stones for many years after, and on such as were carried thence and kept dry, the drops of blood were visible, of a crimson colour, twenty years after. After this shower of blood, broke out the Great Plague, the Dutch and the French wars, and the burning of the City of London."

Nowadays, three hundred years later, men no longer believe that Nature gives warning of terrible disasters to come. But who knows? Calamities strike in cycles, and the heavens might once again rain blood upon St. Dennis and Nanpean. Until that day, the clay-worker will continue to blast and excavate, the wanderer to stare in fascination upon this strange white world of pyramid and pool.

Chapter Twelve

THE BRONTË HERITAGE

THREE sisters, Charlotte, Emily and Anne Brontë, were born and brought up in Yorkshire. Their novels became famous: *Jane Eyre* and *Wuthering Heights* are classics of English literature. Yorkshire people, very rightly, are proud of the three sisters, claiming that childhood and adolescence in a lonely moorland parish, with little influence from the world outside, set imagination working and turned them into novelists. The background was Haworth and the Yorkshire moors, and the tales they heard as children, satisfying their appetite for everything original and strange, were local tales, scraps of history and folk-lore told them by Tabby, the devoted servant who cooked and cared for them.

Their father, the Rev. Patrick Brontë, was an Irishman from County Down, their mother, Maria Branwell, a Cornishwoman from Penzance. Environment can help mould a child into a writer or an artist, but the seed of imagination must first be planted by hereditary factors, then fertilised, nurtured and fed from the same source.

Thousands of visitors travel every year to Haworth Parsonage museum in Yorkshire, walk through the home where the children scribbled their early stories and later wrote their famous novels. The visitors stare out of the windows at the churchyard full of tombs, and venture possibly to the moors at the back of the parsonage, remembering enough of the Brontë story to know that the children's father was Rector of Haworth parish, that their mother died when they were small, and that their mother's sister, Elizabeth Branwell, came to take her place and minister to the household. She was said to dislike the Yorkshire climate and regret her native town, yet she lived at Haworth for twenty-one years until her death in 1842, devoting herself to her brother-in-law and his motherless family.

The four surviving children, Charlotte, Emily, Anne and the brother Branwell, had a Cornish mother whom they barely re-membered, and a Cornish aunt to instruct them in their most formative years. This heritage played an undoubted part in the development of later genius, and if Emily Brontë, and *Wuthering Heights*, will always be associated with the Yorkshire moors it must not be forgotten that both her mother and her aunt had on their own doorstep, through childhood and adolescence, the wild moorland scenery, the stories and the legends, of West Penwith.

Elizabeth Branwell, born in 1776, and her sister Maria, born in 1783, were two of the eleven children of Thomas Branwell and Anne Carne, both of Penzance. Thomas Branwell was a prosperous merchant and a councillor to the corporation. He owned property in and about the town, and was much respected. His family grew up in a house overlooking Mount's Bay and St. Michael's Mount, but towards the latter part of his life he moved to 25 Chapel Street,

Thomas Branwell moved to 25 Chapel Street, Penzance.

higher in the town, near to St. Mary's church or chapel, later, when it was rebuilt in 1834, to become the parish church of Penzance.

Penzance, at the latter part of the eighteenth century, was not only a busy market-town but a flourishing seaport, and one of the coinage towns for tin. The old town had been sacked and burnt to ashes by the Spaniards in 1595, and the new town that grew up upon the site had many handsome buildings of brick and stone, with a fine centre street climbing from the quay to the market place halfway up the hill. Market day, when Elizabeth and Maria Branwell were young women, was a gay affair. The market house was still standing, and the farmers and their wives used to gather on the steps, having ridden in from the surrounding countryside. The fisherwomen wearing scarlet cloaks and broad felt hats would scream their wares to the passers-by, the ladies of the gentry and the merchants' wives who did their own marketing.

These ladies of Penzance were famous for their headdresses, which would become caught in the crooks of the bars hanging overhead between the market-stalls. There was one belle whose "tête," as it was called, became notorious, an erection of ribbons, laces and a cushion, all piled together on the top of her head. Rumour had it that she left her headdress undisturbed too long, and because of a headache was obliged to send for the doctor, who, unravelling the contraption, found a nest of young mice within it and a quantity of fly-blows. The lady was forced to shave her head, but she kept the hair and had it made into a wig, which, as ill-luck had it, caught in one of the market-crooks, and her bald pate was revealed to all and sundry in the market place.

Possibly Elizabeth Branwell's auburn curls, smiled at by her nieces up in Yorkshire and by their friend Ellen Nussey, who remarked upon them in after years, were worn under her large mob cap in memory of that earlier Penzance vogue of girlhood days. "She wore caps large enough for half-a-dozen of the present fashion, and a front of light auburn curls over her forehead," wrote Miss Nussey. "She talked a great deal about her younger days; the gaieties of her dear native town, Penzance, in Cornwall; the social life she used to recall with regret; she gave one the idea that she had been a belle among her own home acquaintances. She took snuff out of a very pretty gold snuff-box, which she sometimes presented to you with a little laugh, as if she enjoyed the slight shock visible in your countenance."

If Miss Branwell liked to shock her nieces and their Yorkshire friend, she must have enjoyed the high jinks in Penzance on Midsummer Eve, when she and her sister Maria would watch the youths parade the streets with burning torches made out of a piece of old sail doubled and dipped in tar, then nailed to the end of a stick and lighted. These banners were swung around the head, and as darkness set in the torchbearers became wilder and noisier; tar-barrels were set alight, bonfires blazed in the middle of the streets, candles were burnt on the doorsteps of the houses. As soon as the fires began to burn low the young people, boys and girls, ran through the streets calling "An eye! An eye!", forming long lines, hand clasping hand, the last two in line raising their arms to make an arch through which the rest ran singing. It is tempting to think of the Miss Branwells dancing wild-eyed through the streets with their companions, but, even if they only watched the hilarity from behind curtained windows, at least they shared in the gaieties of uninhibited Penzance, for the following day, being Midsummer Day, was devoted to "universal idling, water parties, and the Quay fair."

There were, however, more sinister happenings in Chapel Street when the Miss Branwells were growing up, for the neighbouring house was haunted, and not only the house but the orchards and garden surrounding it. The story was so well known amongst the inhabitants of Chapel Street that Elizabeth Branwell could hardly have failed to tell it to her nieces and nephew on winter evenings up in Yorkshire, when the young family gathered in the dining-room for tea.

The house was a mansion then, belonging to an elderly lady called Mrs. Baines. The garden, and especially the orchard, were of some size, planted with fine apple trees, and, fearing thieves, Mrs. Baines commanded her serving-man to keep watch upon her property by night. She was not entirely satisfied with his performance as sentry, and one evening walked out into the orchard herself, and finding him, as she believed, absent, shook down a quantity of apples to teach him a lesson when he returned. Unfortunately she had misjudged her man, who had fallen asleep under one of her precious trees. Thinking he heard the suspected thieves he leapt to his feet with a cry, and discharged his weapon, an old blunderbuss, into his mistress.

"I'm murdered, I'm murdered," shrieked the wretched woman, falling to the ground like one of her own apples, and although her injuries were not thought to be severe she never recovered from the fall, and shortly afterwards died.

From that moment the orchard was said to be haunted by her ghost. The inhabitants of Chapel Street, passing the property, swore that they saw her of an evening walking beneath the trees, dressed in her short silk mantle, with long lace ruffles hanging from her elbows and a lace cap upon her head, and carrying in her right hand a gold-headed cane. No one dared enter the orchard and the apples were left to rot upon the trees. Sometimes, it was said, she would flutter up from the garden like an old hen flying before the wind, and would perch herself upon the wall, her spindly legs and high-heeled shoes visible beneath her petticoats. No one could be found to live in the house, for she would walk from room to room, rattling the furniture, or would be seen, when darkness fell, a shadowy form peering from the windows, shaking an angry fist.

A ghost-layer was finally sent for, a parson named Singleton, famous for exorcizing spirits, and he was somehow successful in luring the restless Mrs. Baines away from her house and orchard to the sands on the western side of the harbour, where she remained until the seas carried her away. The house, however, remained unlet, and for years afterwards the neighbours said they could hear the sound of her spinning-wheel turning in one of the rooms upstairs.

Mrs. Baines was not the only ghost to walk in Chapel Street. The churchyard of St. Mary's chapel near by was also shunned, for a phantom dressed in white was seen to wander amongst the tombs. But an even more fearful apparition was said to trouble the churchyard of a neighbouring parish, where a man lay buried who had died of poisoning. His wife had been convicted of his murder and duly hanged, her guilt certain when the corpse was disinterred for examination and enough arsenic found to have killed three men. It was not the wretched victim who haunted the churchyard but the spectre of the murderess herself, dressed in a winding-sheet with the mark of the rope around her swollen neck. She would be seen spade in hand on stormy nights standing upon her husband's grave, doomed forever more horribly to imitate those who had disturbed the coffin and proved her guilt.

These stories of Penzance, with the legend of Penrose near Sennen only a few miles distant, were enough to send the Brontë children creeping to bed with imagination blazing, to look out upon their own churchyard at Haworth, and the Yorkshire moors behind the parsonage, with anticipation and delicious fear.

The climate indeed was harsher in the north, with bitter cold and frequent snowfalls in the winter, causing their aunt to keep within doors and click about the stone floors of the parsonage in pattens, continually lamenting the warm damp days of Penzance far away in the south-west. When it came to comparing countrysides she also had the advantage over the children, offering them the wide sweep of Mount's Bay and the whole Land's End peninsula, the fishing-villages of Newlyn, Mousehole and St. Ives, besides the rugged grandeur of the moors of West Penwith, crowned with ancient quoits and granite tombs. These were rivals in their loneliness and beauty to Oakenden Stones on Crow Hill, familiar to her Yorkshire-bred nieces and nephew. Ponden Kirk, a rock with a hole driven through the centre, high up on Stanbury Moor and a favourite climb of the young Brontës, had the same legends and traditions as the Mên-an-Tol stone in Madron parish near Penzance. To crawl through the stone cured all ills, and ensured an early marriage into the bargain. The rocks and stones of those Yorkshire moors, which became famous as Penistone Crags in *Wuthering Heights*, have the same austerity, the same remote splendour as those of West Penwith; to a walker who

162

knows both the only difference is that in Cornwall the sea wind blows upon him from all sides.

"*Wuthering Heights*," wrote Charlotte Brontë after Emily's death, "was hewn in a wild workshop, with simple tools, out of homely materials. The statuary found a granite block on a solitary moor; gazing thereon, he saw how from the crag might be elicited a head, savage, swart, sinister; a form moulded with at least one element of grandeur – power. He wrought with a rude chisel, and from no model but the vision of his meditations."

This vision, nurtured by personal knowledge and observation of the Yorkshire landscape, was drawn from within, part of the heritage bequeathed to Emily Brontë from the Cornwall she had never seen or known.

In 1812 Maria Branwell, aged twenty-nine and still living with her unmarried sisters in Penzance, left for a visit to Yorkshire to stay with an uncle, Mr. Joseph Fennell, a Methodist preacher and Governor of Woodhouse Grove Wesleyan Academy. Here she met the Rev. Patrick Brontë, son of an Irish weaver, six years older than herself, who was curate at Hartshead near Dewsbury. They fell in love and were married the same year, on December 29, at Guiseley church, near Bradford. Her family did not attend the wedding, for on that same day Maria's second sister Charlotte married a cousin, Joseph Branwell, at Madron church, then the parish church of Penzance, and famous for that wishing-well in whose spring waters mothers used to plunge their naked infants.

Maria Branwell never returned to Cornwall. Three years after their marriage her husband exchanged his living at Hartshead for that of Thornton, and in 1820 he became vicar of Haworth. Their six children, all born within eight years at Hartshead and Thornton, took their toll of Maria's health. She was already a sick woman when she arrived in Haworth, but fortitude and love for her husband and children helped her to conceal the pain that was already part of her. She became dangerously ill with cancer the following January, and hovered between life and death for seven long months until she died on September 15, 1821. Little is known of her character and personality. No record shows whether she regretted Cornwall, and letters written to her family and friends in Penzance have never come to light.

That she loved her former home is evident in an extract from a letter written to Patrick Brontë before their marriage. "Unless my love for you were very great, how could I so contentedly give up my home and all my friends – a home I love so much that I have often thought nothing could bribe me to renounce it for any length of time together, and friends with whom I have been so long accustomed to share all the vicissitudes of joy and sorrow?" Nor could she have easily submitted to a husband's authority. "For some years I have been perfectly my own mistress, subject to no *control* whatever – so far from it, that my sisters who are many years older than myself, and even my dear mother, used to consult me in every case of importance."

Here is Cornish individuality and pride, both qualities that would be strong in her daughter Emily in years to come. Even her last months, described by her husband in a letter to a friend, show the same strange withdrawal to inner solitude with which Emily Brontë pained her family twenty-seven years later. "Just at that time death seemed to have laid his hand on my dear wife in a manner which threatened her with speedy dissolution. She was cold and silent and seemed hardly to notice what was passing around her. A few weeks afterwards her sister, Miss Branwell, arrived, and afforded great comfort to my mind which has been the case ever since, by sharing my labours and my sorrows, and behaving as an affectionate mother to my children. At the earliest opportunity I called in different medical gentlemen to visit the beloved sufferer, but all their skill was in vain. Death pursued her unrelentingly. Her constitution was enfeebled, and her frame wasted daily; and after above seven months of more agonising pain than I ever saw anyone endure she fell asleep in Jesus, and her soul took its flight to the mansions of glory. During many years she walked with God, but the great enemy, envying her life of holiness, often disturbed her mind in the last conflict . . ."

Elizabeth Branwell remained to share the labours and sorrows until her own death. There is no record that she, any more than her sister Maria, ever returned to her native Penzance.

These two Cornishwomen, bred to a different way of life in the market-town where their family was well known, neither of them young when they left home, brought their own spirit of indomitable courage to the parsonage on the Yorkshire moors, to live amongst people who, however kindly and hospitable, were apt to think that southerners were "soft." Penzance, to Yorkshire eyes, was a watering-place for the genteel who had grown prosperous by trade, who had never done a hard day's work in a mill, and Cornwall a far-off county pleasantly surrounded by blue sea, with primroses blooming in the hedges, where it never snowed. They were mistaken, but it was not their fault. Northerners seldom crossed the Tamar in the early nineteenth century. Another hundred years would pass before the annual holiday became the fashion, and Yorkshire folk in their thousands travelled south-west to discover Cornwall for themselves.

Now there is no barrier to understanding. The visitor from the north, remembering with a certain nostalgia the idle looms and vacant mills of his own homeland, can look with sympathy upon the desolate Cornish mines. Here he will find the moorland scenery that he loves and knows, the heather and the scrub, even the sudden storms and driving rain. Lovers of the Brontë novels, familiar with the Parsonage museum where the sisters wrote their books, can look about them in Penzance and West Penwith with knowledge ripened, much of what had puzzled them hitherto made suddenly plain. Did not the Brontë sisters with their brother Branwell invent islands, when they were children? Were there not fortresses on Emily's kingdom of Gondal, and dungeons, and civil wars? Did this all come from imagination, from something they had read in books, or from tales they had been told?

St. Michael's Mount, dwelling of hermits, of Benedictine monks, of feudal barons and rebellious earls, stronghold of the Royalist Sir Arthur Basset in the Civil War until he surrendered it to Parliament in

165

St. Michael's Mount.

1646, and later, impoverished, sold it to one of the Parliamentary leaders, John St. Aubyn – whose descendant, another Sir John, modernised the whole structure into a family residence in 1760 – dominated Mount's Bay when Elizabeth Branwell was a girl, as it does today. She would have seen it, fair day or foul, from her childhood home in Penzance, and this rocky islet, with the causeway leading to it at low tide, surrounded by the sea which barred all travellers when the tide was full, would have been the strongest and the most precious of her memories.

What dreams of captives and of castaways, what cries from dungeons, what legends of storm-tossed mariners this "little anti-quated lady with the auburn curls" must have engendered in the minds of the listening children long ago, to awaken in them that narrative power, that sense of the dramatic which is such a part of the Cornish character, moulding them, unconsciously, to the shape of their maternal forebears long since dead, individualists one and all, rugged as the granite on the moors of West Penwith.

Chapter Thirteen

PORTS AND PILCHARDS

IN the old days, if a Cornishman was not streaming for tin, mining it underground or in some way getting his living from the soil, the odds were that his home was in one of the numerous small villages clustering by the sea's edge and that, like his ancestors before him, he gained his livelihood by fishing. Although every time he put to sea he could be said to take his life in his hands, it was in many ways a less hazardous occupation than digging for tin. Every tinner had a gambler's streak inside him. The precious ore might or might not be found in those gravel streams beside the granite, or underground. If he was successful there was a chance, if not of fortune, at least of a period of stability while stream or mine continued to be productive; if unsuccessful there was nothing for it but privation for himself and his family, until he tried again and struck it lucky.

The fisherman faced no such challenge. The fish were in the sea, and would not fail him. Misadventure to himself and his companions, to his boat and nets, was the danger that encompassed him, and could with reasonable precautions be avoided. The fact that many a fisherman was drowned and his boat smashed was due, not to ignorance, but to the daring and courage flowing in his blood, as it did in that of his miner brother. Wise in the weather, he knew that when the wind backed with the changing tide there could be increase in wind and sea, and the smallest miscalculation in the timing of his return to harbour might spell danger, even disaster; but the desire to bring home a full catch and beat the weather won over prudence every time. As for the fish, centuries of experience had taught him what shoals were to be expected and in what season.

The great mainstay of the trade was a fish rather smaller than a herring and slightly larger than a sardine, met with only round the coasts of Cornwall and sometimes off the south-west of Ireland – the Cornish pilchard. Pilchards travel, or more correctly used to travel, from the Atlantic, round the Scilly isles towards the Cornish coast, in mid-July, remaining in coastal waters until November and December. Cornishmen were presumably catching pilchards from the earliest days, for from time immemorial it was their staple diet, eaten fresh in summer months and salted down for winter. Carew, in his *Survey of Cornwall*, described how they were caught, a method hardly changed from before his day in the seventeenth century down to our own times. There were certain small differences according to district, but the timing was the same, the expectation of the shoals in August, when every man, woman and child would be prepared for the annual excitement and hard labour.

The first step was to post a look-out called a "huer" on the cliff-head – the word deriving from "hevva," a shoal of fish. Armed with a furze bush, he would stand in his vantage-place watching for a dark shadow on the sea, heralding the shoals. Meanwhile boats, men and nets would be waiting on the shore. As soon as the dark cloud rippling the water's surface was observed the huer shouted "Hevva! Hevva!", frantically waving his furze bush to right or left, signalling the progress of the pilchards as they swam forward in their massed thousands. The boats were launched and the "seine" was shot, the object being to entrap the entire shoal, much as sheep are driven into a pen. A second net, known as the "tucking" net, was then attached to the first, the whole contraption forming a circle; the fish were virtually imprisoned by this process. The great event for those on shore was the hauling to the surface of the leaping, writhing fish, as the men in the seine boats heaved in the tucking-net. Any boat capable of holding fish waited beside the net, and suddenly the whole surface became alive, sizzling and boiling like a cauldron, the frantic pilchards striving to escape the ensnaring net and the fleet of

Opposite: *One of the small villages clustering by the sea's edge.*

boats. Sometimes the shoals would be so great that, even before the seine boats were in position and the nets shot, the fish would be driven of their own volition close inshore and up upon the beach, there to gasp and flap like drowning seamen, and be thrown into every available bucket and basket.

The next procedure was to get them, in carts and barrows, from the beach to the salting-house, where the women were waiting to pile them up on layers of salt. They would remain in salt, or "in bulk," as it used to be called, for some five or six weeks, during which time the residue of oil, salt and water that dripped into the stone wells below would serve a further purpose, the salt, water and offal turned into manure, the oil clarified and sold. The revenue from these by-products was enough to pay for the services of the "seiners." As for the pilchards themselves, those that were not sold locally and kept for the winter – and every household had its large store of salted pilchards – were washed and packed in hogsheads and then sent to the nearest seaport for dispatch abroad, since, outside Cornwall, there was little demand for pilchards in England. Italy and Spain were the chief markets, the main reason being their strict observance of Lent fasting.

Pilchards were also caught by drift-nets further offshore, as were mackerel, another seasonal fish which was plentiful in the summer months, coming sometimes in shoals close inshore much as the pilchards did, or fished by hook and line in a fast-moving boat. Crabs and lobsters were sought in the summer too, the pots sunk near to rocks and left for a few days, if the weather promised well, before being lifted and brought ashore. Cod and ling were caught on the long-line during the winter months, whiting, pollack and bass throughout the year, but every fisherman was a specialist in his particular sea-bed and the depth of water in which he fished.

The inshore fishermen with their little boats, who came from the smaller villages and coves, kept mostly to home waters, but the venturers in quest of herring far from land had larger boats with fair-sized crews, and would sail as far as Ireland and the north of

170

Scotland, returning down the east coast of England and so to the Channel. St. Ives harbour, shaped like a horse-shoe on the western side of the sweeping bay leading to Hayle estuary, was protected from the prevailing south-westerly gales, and, although the harbour dried out at low tide and seas ran shallow over the sandy bay, boats could fish offshore and up the north coast when those in Channel fishing-ports and coves were weather-bound. St. Ives dominated north-coast fishing, her only rival, Padstow, up the silting Camel estuary. Smaller harbours, Boscastle, Port Isaac, Newquay, were mere villages and never serious competitors.

Channel fishing-ports had the advantage of generally deeper water, some of them with inner harbours, the outer walls giving better protection when seas were rough. The great gulf, Mount's Bay, between Land's End and Lizard Point, was fine fishing-ground, the chief ports being Newlyn and its smaller neighbour Mousehole. Porthleven west of the Loe Bar was another harbour, with a fleet of locally-built boats, able to withstand the roughest weather, and every cove west and east of Lizard Point was proud to call itself a fishing-village – Mullion, Cadgwith, Coverack, Porthoustock and Port-hallow, as far as the Helford and Fal estuaries.

East of the Fal to Dodman Point, St. Mawes, Portscatho, Portloe and Portholland all lived by fishing, while east of the Dodman Mevagissey, Gorran, Polperro and Looe dominated the scene up to Rame Head and Plymouth Sound. Fowey, with its deep-water harbour, was a seaport first and foremost, and never possessed a fishing-fleet of its own.

The arrival of the railway was a tremendous boon to Cornish fishermen. The men of St. Ives, Newlyn and Mousehole could pack their fresh fish off to London by train at Penzance, while Truro, Par and Liskeard served the ports and villages further up-channel. It seemed as if wealth would come at last to those Cornishmen who lived by and from the sea. The hand-to-mouth existence would be over, the annual stand-by for the pilchard harvest no longer the greatest event of the fishing year but part of a seasonal catch. Fishing-boats were built in every port of any size from St.

Ives to Looe, their shape and structure designed to suit local needs.

St. Ives boats were usually double-ended, pointed fore and aft, the narrow stern thus rising easily and offering little resistance to the short-breaking seas in St. Ives Bay. They were of shallow draft, enabling them to squat easily upon the sandy harbour base at low tide. These boats would vary in size and form according to the type of fishing for which they were built. The larger vessels were used for drifting, following mackerel from March to June, then going right offshore into the Atlantic after herrings, staying away sometimes until the autumn. The smaller boats carrying the seine nets for pilchards were harbour-based. A hundred years ago there were some sixty or more luggers – called so because of the four-cornered lug-sail bent fore and aft upon a single yard – and some two-hundred-and-fifty seine boats, all in St. Ives harbour. The Mount's Bay boats were also double-enders, but beyond the Lizard, where harbours were deeper and conditions both in port and at sea differed, the Falmouth Quay Punt became popular, a vessel with a square transom stern and a deep keel. Boats similar to this were also built at Mevagissey and Looe.

The fifty years between the coming of the railway and the close of the nineteenth century saw the peak of the Cornish fishing trade. Those indefatigable walkers to the Land's End, Wilkie Collins, Walter White and Alphonse Esquiros, found themselves knee-deep in fish when they arrived in Newlyn and St. Ives, Alphonse Esquiros in particular being disillusioned by what he thought at first must be a Greek village turning too swiftly to an offensive-smelling pilchard port.

"St. Ives," he wrote gloomily, "does not gain by being seen more closely. The more beautiful its position is, the more do its narrow, winding streets appear made to sadden visitors and dispel illusions. It is a thorough fishing town. Nearly all the houses have stone steps outside, leading to the first floors, where the families live, while the ground-floors are occupied by the fish-cellars. The latter spread through the inhabited part of the houses exhalations which are far from agreeable, especially in the pilchard season; but the fishermen

"Houses at St. Ives" by Alfred Wallis.

scent in this fish an odour quite as good as another – the fragrance of gain and prosperity."

Alphonse Esquiros' *Cornwall and Its Coasts* was written in 1865. Some thirty years of "gain and prosperity" were to gladden the fishermen's hearts before the decline began. The pilchards were the first to desert the Cornish shores. What migratory laws compelled them to change course no one could say, but soon after the turn of the century the mass invasion every summer ceased, the seine boats waited in vain, the huer's cry was no longer heard, the drifters had to go far out to sea in search of the wayward shoals. The last great catches of pilchards close inshore were made in St. Ives Bay in 1905 and 1907.

Worse was to come, for by the start of the twentieth century Cornishmen found they were not alone in fishing their own waters.

Drifters from the North Sea came to the south-west, east-coast men from Lowestoft, Yarmouth and other ports, with bigger, more powerful boats, joined by French trawlers from across the Channel. The east-coast men installed engines in their boats while the Cornishman was still dependent on his lug-sail. Fierce competition not only cluttered the market but spoilt the fishing-grounds. The First World War, with its call-up of younger men, was a further severe blow to fishermen in Cornwall, and, although between the wars there was some revival of the trade, competition increased, and today, despite diesel engines, the twelve-mile limit for foreign trawlers, government subsidies and a courageous effort on the part of those Cornish fishermen determined to make a success of their old calling, prospects are doubtful still.

It is depressing to discover that the veritable fleet of seine boats seen in St. Ives harbour by Alphonse Esquiros in 1865 existed no longer in 1924 – all of them had been broken up for firewood. Much the same thing happened in other fishing-ports, Mevagissey, Polperro and Looe, harbours once packed with fishing-vessels moored stem to stern. Slowly the larger boats fell into disuse, decks rotting, sides blistering, gear rusting, their despondent owners idle on the quay.

When I lived in Bodinnick, Fowey, some ten years before the outbreak of the Second World War, the small fleets putting out to sea from their fishing-villages were a handsome sight, line upon line of boats from Looe and Polperro travelling westward on a summer's evening. Later, when it became dark, and I leant out from the hatch-way window overlooking Fowey harbour, their lights would wink on the far horizon as they had doubtless done through centuries, the boats crewed by the same families, generation after generation, father to son. I was at that time the proud possessor of a Quay Punt built at Slades Yard, Polruan, where schooners had been built in days gone by, and fired by romantic thoughts, ignorant of fishing and of sailing, I invested in a trawl to cast over her square transom stern, with visions of mighty catches to bring home to port. The resulting haul was too often rayfish, uneatable, or squid that spat an inky fluid when thrown upon the deck, but salty hands scarred by wet rope made me feel myself a seaman, and my heart rejoiced even as my stomach heaved.

Later my husband and I bought a fishing-boat from Mevagissey, built originally at Porthleven in Mount's Bay. We called her *Restless*, and although she never sailed east of the Hamble river in the Solent, or west of Helford river in our own Cornish waters, we thought ourselves mariners after our own fashion, at one, as we fished for pleasure and our supper, with those who fished for livelihood, hailing them as comrades as we passed down-channel, engaged in the same deeply satisfying task.

Restless, like many another Cornish fishing-boat, ended her days a hulk upon a beach, a stranded victim of enforced neglect during the six years of the second war. There are some six vessels of her size

"PZ 134" by Christopher Wood.

TOWNER GALLERY, EASTBOURNE.

today in Mevagissey harbour. The livelier undecked Mevagissey "toshers" are more popular both with the fishermen, who can manoeuvre between fishing-grounds and port with greater speed, and with the summer visitors, who, packed tighter than the pilchards they replace, chug-chug seaward for a "trip round the bay."

Fishing, of course, continues. Crab, lobster, crayfish are sought after by the managers of guest-houses and hotels. Sole, plaice and salmon (the upper reach of Fowey river is, or was, a happy hunting-ground for this, and his smaller relative salmon peal) are also in demand for the visitor's dining-table, with whiting – generally a glut of these – taking second place, while mackerel, best consumed as soon as caught, and pollack, described by a non-enthusiast as tasting like cotton-wool with pins in it, still content the less fastidious native palate.

Pilchards are no longer salted down for the winter by the Cornish housewife, but they are still caught, even if they do not swarm in thousands close inshore, and a canning industry started a thriving trade in Mevagissey before the second war, exporting to Italy and other Mediterranean countries, even as far as Egypt's Alexandria. Here, commanding his battalion of Grenadiers in 1937, my husband, delighted at the discovery, forced tins of them upon his reluctant troops, who, sweating in temperatures approaching the nineties, would have preferred to quench their thirst and risk dysentery with the Egyptian melon. We proffered pilchards at our dinner-table to unsuspecting cotton kings and their wives, who ate them unprotesting. They were a change, after all, from the invariable curried rice and prawns. The gesture may not have added to the wealth of the Mevagissey canners, but it satisfied our own nostalgia.

Today the Mevagissey canning factories talk of closing down, not, they say, because pilchards are no more but because the fishermen do not care to look for them, declaring that it is not worth their while. They can make more money filling their boats with summer visitors. The argument continues, but if the canning factories close it will be another sign of the changing way of life in Cornish fishing-ports.

St. Ives and Newlyn – especially Newlyn – struggle for survival against the competition of the North Sea drifters, but the boy leaving school no longer wants to follow his father's, or more often his grandfather's, trade. Even bigger boats with powerful diesel engines are not the inducement they would have been twenty, thirty years ago. There is a reluctance to go to sea when fish, however plentiful, show a poor market return.

Killing fish for kicks and not consumption is a profitable affair, and shark-hunting is the new "status sport" around the Cornish coasts. Powerful boats with powerful engines are necessary for this venture, fitted with the latest landing gear, and the visitor with money to throw around can fancy himself in the role of a white hunter on safari, the safari being at sea, and the game the inedible shark whose skin is not even worth the stripping. The excuse given in support of this exercise by its participators is that sharks are the natural enemies of fishermen and destroy their nets. If so, it is only of late years that this fact has been discovered. Perhaps the porpoise will be the next quarry on the sportsman's list, his lazy tumble on a calm day in summer providing an easy target for shot-gun or harpoon.

Water-skiing is another bait to catch the affluent tourist. Any motor-boat will serve, providing it has a good turn of speed, and can bump out of a cove at full throttle and then make a circle in the open sea without cutting off the bobbing heads of nearby swimmers. If this palls there is always under-water fishing, when the swimmer, suitably attired in rubber-proofed clothing and diving head-piece, can venture to the depths and spear a flat-fish, dozing on the sea- or river-bed – a sport which is hardly popular with the local fishermen, for whom fish are their livelihood.

In port, whether it be St. Ives or Mevagissey, Looe or Polperro, the visitor who does not go afloat has his tastes catered for in other ways. He can park his car, jammed with a hundred others on the quays, then stroll in the confined space and stare in trinket-booths. "Corn-wall," declared an enthusiast not long ago, "must become the playground of all England." He was doubtless a man of vision.

The fishing-villages of Cornwall might seem fated to exploitation, like those of Spain's Costa Brava, were it not for one factor, the Cornish climate. Holiday-makers, no matter their nationality, seek above all else the sun. Playgrounds do not thrive under the rain. Clay-workers, quarriers, tinners, even farmers and market-gardeners may grumble but do not heed a rising wind and steady drizzle. Fishermen can put to sea unless a gale blows. But the tourist, shivering in shorts or cotton frock, will in the end look for consolation elsewhere.

Meanwhile, elderly natives by birth or by adoption can live on memories. When coves and beaches covered with ice-cream cartons, cigarette-packets, corn-plasters and contraceptives daunt the intending swimmer, and the sound of radio, speed-boat and barking dogs pollutes the air, I travel back some five-and-fifty years to 1912, watching and listening to other, fiercer sights and to other more sinister sounds. I am five years old, fast asleep in bed beside my elder sister on a summer's evening in a house in Mullion cove. Our parents, like other holiday-makers before and since, disgusted by the weather, have fled to France, leaving us in the charge of temporary governess, nurse and nursery-maid. Suddenly we are awakened by our keepers bursting into our room in disarray, laughing, gesticulating, their decorum vanished. They drag us from our beds, thrusting coats over our nightgowns, forcing sand-shoes on to our feet. What has happened? Is it fire, is it flood? What are the shouting and the crying outside our windows? They hurry us from the house to the cliff's edge, and all Mullion is assembled there, pointing, shouting, staring down to the troubled waters in the cove. Governess, nurse and nursemaid, visitors like ourselves to Cornwall, who have never in the sanctum of nursery or schoolroom soiled their hands with stinking fish, scream in our ears "The pilchards are in . . . the pilchards are in!"

I stare bewildered, frightened, fascinated, down from the cliff-head to what seems in the fading light the gleaming underworld. The

Opposite: *The gleaming underworld.*

water is a seething mass of fish struggling to escape, and men in boats and on shore are laughing, shouting, like the watchers on the cliffs, and someone beyond us cries in a high-pitched voice. I look up at the governess for reassurance, but the fever has seized her too, along with the nurse and nursemaid, and they start to run with us along the cliffs towards the crier, laughing, waving their arms, the governess's hair, usually fastened in a bun, streaming down her back. My sister, highly strung, is near to tears. I find myself stirred, not so much by the scene about and below us as by the extraordinary behaviour of our mentors. Is it because our mother, whose word is law, has gone away? Is all this lovely folly a bid for freedom, showing that grown-ups, as well as children, seek escape?

Pilchards . . . pilchards . . . pilchards . . . The primitive turmoil of a Cornish world gone mad. We are no longer frowned upon, imprisoned in our silly beds. Here at last is licence, liberty, a strange ecstasy never before experienced, bringing the discovery that governess, nurse and nursemaid are not infallible. I run beside them, secretly mocking their fall from grace, yet filled with a sudden wild delight.

Chapter Fourteen

FAIR-TRADERS

SMUGGLING is a word that too often suggests men with black patches over their eyes, clad in striped jerseys and stockinged caps, dragging kegs of brandy and rum into secret caves. Like King Arthur and his knights galloping across moorlands to Tintagel, the word is immediately associated with Cornwall, despite the fact that the practice was universal up and down the English coast. Desire to thwart the law is a basic human instinct, going back into the mists of time. Rules, it is said, are made to break, and the most honest of persons feels a tingle of pleasure if he succeeds, by some cunning means, in outwitting authority.

The Cornish, never a docile people, saw the possibilities of the game in the twelfth century, when the tinners assembled at the coinage towns, mingling with officers of the law, London merchants, traders, and all the petty fry who expected a cut out of the proceedings. If the price offered was likely to disappoint, and the tinner was already in debt, it was easy enough to dispose of some of the stuff while it was still in the blowing-house, before being taken to the coinage town to be weighed, stamped and sold. The tinner had his "contacts," as they would be called today, travelling tinkers and pedlars, who would pay an agreed price, and then pass the tin on to seamen in the nearest port to sell on the Continent. It was one way of insuring himself against loss in a trade that was a gamble at the best of times.

As the industry expanded in later centuries the practice grew, a steady pilfering taking place at the streaming-site or mine, mostly by the poorer tinner to augment his wage once the landowner took charge, and always with the same end in view, to get rid of what he had to foreign seamen, or come to an arrangement with the master of a Cornish vessel bound for a Continental port. For the owners of these vessels it was a convenient form of trade between wars, with the tin conveniently hidden beneath a legitimate cargo due for discharge in Brittany, Portugal or the Mediterranean. They would return with a cargo equally contraband – brandy, tea, salt, the last being a necessity for the pilchard fishermen, who found themselves hard hit when the salt tax was introduced in the latter part of the eighteenth century.

Smuggling, or fair-trading, as it was called with nice distinction, came easily to the Cornish people, because many of them who lived by the coast, especially in ports like Fowey, Looe, Penryn on the Fal and Penzance, had, through the fifteenth and sixteenth centuries, deployed themselves in piracy. Here again, the pantomime image of the black patch and stockinged cap mocks a practice that was in reality a legacy of the Hundred Years' War, when Cornish ports supplied transport ships to carry Plantagenet armies across the Channel. The owners of these ships found it profitable to attack and board a French vessel, subdue her crew, loot her contents and either sink her or bring her home as prize.

The cessation of the war made little difference to such expeditions: the taste remained. The gentlemen of England who had not fought at Agincourt beside Henry V were certainly not abed, at least in Cornwall. They were somewhere on the high seas, harassing French ships or lying in wait for them off the Normandy coast. The gallants of Fowey, famous for their marauding sorties, found themselves trumped on one occasion, when a Breton fleet in 1457 attacked their town in the absence of the leading citizen, Thomas Treffry, whose home, Place House, was courageously defended by his wife while half the town was in flames.

A hundred years later, although the harassing continued, the target was the Spaniard, not the Frenchman, with the Killigrew family from Arwennack on the Fal the principal "privateers", the name given to those gentlemen of fortune who had government

Place House, courageously defended by Thomas Treffry's wife, while half the town was in flames.

permission to use their armed vessels against the common enemy. Privateer or pirate, the distinction between the two was narrow. Privateering was permitted, piracy frowned upon by high authority, but before war broke out between England and Spain the Killigrews ignored the frown, along with other Cornish gentlemen, and had the satisfaction of filling their cellars with Spanish booty.

They did not always have things their own way. Retaliation came from others of the same persuasion when the Spanish war was over. Pirates from Algeria and Morocco, more professional than the Cornish, descended upon Mount's Bay and terrified the people of Penzance. They even sailed up-channel as far as Looe, seizing eighty ships from that small port alone.

During the Commonwealth, and after the Restoration of the monarchy, a reconstructed Navy kept foreigners at bay, and piracy, as a lucrative sport for Cornishmen, was over. Privateers became fair-traders. The vessels that had formerly harassed the French and Spanish coasts slipped into foreign ports on a new, more friendly basis, in search of contraband. It was a pursuit, a game, which all enjoyed, with little distinction between persons of varying social status. The tinner down on his luck, the fisherman in quest of salt, the squire who liked his brandy, the squire's lady who dressed herself in lace, even the vicar of the parish, often a relative of the squire – each participated, after his own fashion, in this doubtful though delicious flouting of the law. The necessity of sharing hazards made a link between all the parties. The owner of the vessel, trader or fishing-boat had to evade the Revenue cutters while he was at sea, and dispose of his contraband before arriving in his home port. Signals were exchanged between him and the local fishermen. The smaller coves, the narrower inlets, legion round the Cornish coast, were ideal for the purpose, and when wind and tide and moon suited there would be a rendezvous between the vessel and a smaller boat offshore, a transferring of the contraband from one to the other. Then the trading vessel would make for her true destination in all innocence, while her accomplices in the small fishing-boat pulled the stuff ashore.

The next stage of the proceeding was likely to prove more dangerous. The contraband must first be hidden, not necessarily in the inevitable cave of romance and legend, but often in the houses or storerooms of obliging persons living near by, frequently merchants who had access to waggons, or neighbouring farmers, or even the local squire with suitable cellars. The timing was important, for the Excise men were constantly on watch. They had either to be circumvented or lured on a false trail, while the little party carrying contraband shifted their goods from one hiding-place to another for final dispersal.

Excise men were open to bribes. The obliging squire was often a magistrate. Intermarriage amongst the Cornish, making cousins of so many families in village or parish, encouraged loyalty. There was a code of honour amongst fair-traders, certainly within individual districts. What happened in other villages further up or down the coast was another matter, for fair-traders worked a narrow circuit. The only men who moved willingly from one district to another were the tinners, go-betweens in many an escapade.

Each coastal port or fishing village had its local hero, although authentic names are hard to trace today, with many a hearthside story of desperate doings and great struggles between officers of the law and their smuggling opponents passing from family to family, becoming exaggerated and embellished in the process, unconsciously confused with earlier traditions dating back to days of piracy, or legendary happenings lost in the mists of time.

The heyday for the fair-traders was the eighteenth century, when the industrial revolution was upsetting the old tenor of life, fortunes were being made or lost in tin and copper, and society was changing into the "haves" and the "have nots," with the poorer members of it glad enough to participate in any enterprise that might help to fill their bellies, while those already rich were greedy for greater wealth.

Probably the most famous of Cornish smugglers, saluted even for his calling, which was known to all, was John Carter, who ran cargoes between the French coast and his own home above Prussia Cove, an inlet on Mount's Bay east of Cudden Point. He and his brother Harry were great sticklers for discipline and orderly conduct; no man who worked for them was allowed licence of behaviour, and their reputation for honesty was such that the Excise men respected them, declaring that they only took what was their due. John Carter kept a public house, the King of Prussia, and his fish-cellars in the cliffs below the inn were storerooms for contraband. Here he mounted a battery of six-pounders to dispel invaders, and one day let fly with them at a naval sloop-of-war, the *Fairy*, which had ventured too close inshore for his liking. This proved his undoing, temporarily at any rate, for the commander of the sloop sent his men ashore to destroy the battery; but the King of Prussia, as his friends styled him after his own inn, continued to reign until 1807.

Another well-known smuggler, Wellard, owner of the *Happy-Go-Lucky*, had become such a thorn in the flesh of the Excise men that he was banned as an outlaw, for not only did he carry contraband but his vessel was armed. Wellard swore that he would never be taken alive, and for months he eluded capture, sailing well offshore or keeping to the French coast. Samuel Pellow, appointed as Collector of Customs at Falmouth, had to deal with the *Happy-go-Lucky* and six other smuggling cutters and luggers besides, a veritable squadron, mounting some fifty-six guns amongst them. He even surprised a party of his own officers helping to run a cargo of wine in broad daylight, so great was the corruption amongst the Excise men when he took over his appointment.

The *Happy-Go-Lucky* met her fate in April 1786. Two cruisers surprised her one morning at anchor off Mullion Island, west of the Lizard. Her crew slipped their cable and made for sea, and after an hour's battle, fiercely fought, Wellard and his mate were killed and twelve of the crew wounded, while the rest surrendered. The outlawed vessel was taken in tow to Falmouth and the crew imprisoned in Pendennis Castle. Still they were not defeated, and knowing that the civil force was weak in the Castle, and would have to send for a company of soldiers from Plymouth to guard them, they succeeded in breaking out before the soldiers arrived, and managed to rescue those of their wounded comrades who had been lodged in the town – all save one, who was sent up to Newgate Prison in London, and thence for trial.

Another character, of a more questionable nature, was Cruel Coppinger, wrecker, pirate, smuggler, said to roam the north coast between Marsland Mouth and Bude Bay. The Rev. R. S. Hawker, vicar of Morwenstow, wrote of his exploits in both verse and prose, but he was a better romancer than historian, and although the Gull Rock off Marsland Mouth is still pointed out as the scene of Coppinger's final departure from the coast, when he stood upon it, cutlass in hand, signalling to his waiting vessel for the boat's crew to pull inshore through the boiling surf and carry him aboard, the tale has a legendary quality, dating back beyond the eighteenth century and across the border into Devon.

On the opposite side of the peninsula, at Polperro on the Channel coast, the whole village engaged in smuggling, with small thought of dishonesty or shame. It was a part of life in which everyone joined, fisherman, blacksmith, farmer, and the Excise men themselves. Ships were built for the purpose in yards set upon Consona Rocks and the Peak above the harbour, and one vessel was so successful that she made five hundred trips across to the Continent to bring back contraband.

Polperro in the eighteenth century was hardly more than a crevice in the cliff, with its cluster of dwellings by the harbour's edge and a deep winding valley beyond. Cottages and fish-cellars jumbled together made excellent hiding-places for forbidden goods, nor was it a pleasant task for the Excise men to descend into the valley after hearing rumours that a "run" had taken place the night before, there to be faced with a band of angry villagers, many of them armed. On one occasion, hearing that a large number of kegs of brandy were hidden in a certain cellar above Yellow Rock, a force of Excise men marched to Polperro from Fowey, nine miles away. When they reached the harbour and the suspected cellar they found a band of armed smugglers waiting to receive them, with a loaded gun pointing in their direction, ready to fire when the leader gave his signal. The Excise officer thought it best to retire and send for a still stronger force, but when they returned in strength to rush the cellar the kegs had disappeared, despite the fact that the cellar had been watched by posted sentries.

True stories such as these, handed down from father to son, gave rise to the many tales of after-years, of secret passages from cellar to cove, from farmhouse to cave, stoutly upheld along the Cornish coasts by the romantic-minded descendants of those who had plied their doubtful and dangerous practices in days gone by.

Fair-traders who armed their crews and mounted guns upon their ships were hardly to be blamed, for during the Napoleonic wars they

were encouraged by the government to do this very thing, and were commissioned as privateers to seek out the enemy and engage them in battle. It seemed, to the hardy skippers of such vessels and their adventurous crews, the most natural thing in the world to retain their weapons between wars, and make use of them when carrying contraband and challenged by the Revenue officers.

The *Lottery* was a well-known Polperro lugger, famous for her fast sailing qualities, which resisted capture one day in Whitesand Bay east of Looe. Shots were exchanged between her and the craft manned by the Revenue forces, in the course of which a Revenue man was killed. This caused an outcry from authority, and orders were issued to seize every member of the lugger's crew when they finally came ashore. For weeks they remained elusive, visiting their families secretly by night, until one of them, Roger Toms, thinking to save his own skin and be rewarded into the bargain, turned informer, gave himself up, and declared that the fatal shot had been fired by one of his comrades, Tom Potter. The moment his betrayal became known, the people of Polperro were determined upon a common cause, to hide Tom Potter from the authorities, and to get Roger Toms out of the country so that he would not become King's Evidence. The Revenue officers, well aware of what might happen to the informer, kept him aboard their cutter in Polruan opposite Fowey, but Potter's friends induced the informer's wife to go to Polruan and meet her husband there, and persuade him to go with her a mile or so out of the village, where, under cover of darkness, they waylaid him and put him upon a ship bound for Guernsey.

The smugglers now believed themselves secure, with Toms, in Guernsey, unable to make use of his information. Unfortunately he was traced and brought back to Plymouth, while at the same time a detachment of soldiers marched upon Polperro, surprising the luckless Tom Potter hiding in his own cottage, which, unlike those of his neighbours, had no back door to the hills. He was taken to

Opposite: *Cottages and fish-cellars jumbled together made excellent hiding places for forbidden goods.*

London protesting his innocence, but was convicted of murder at the Old Bailey, and hanged. The people of Polperro continued to insist that he was innocent, and that Roger Toms had acted throughout from malice. Whether this was so or not was never proved, but Roger Toms did not dare set foot in Cornwall again, and he died, many years later, a servant in Newgate Prison. Memories are long, and for ever afterwards the name of Roger Toms was a term of reproach along the east Cornish coast.

In 1856, when the Coastguard Act was passed, and the watch on the coasts of England passed to the control of the Admiralty, smuggling came virtually to an end. The great era of fair-trading was over. The general mass of Cornish people, brought up for three

The great era of fair-trading was over.

generations now to Methodism and a stricter observance of the law, when to engage in any pursuit upon a Sunday, let alone fish home waters or put to sea in search of other quarry, was a disgrace and an offence against God's Holy Word, had disciplined themselves to eschew adventure. Respectability was all. Queen Victoria was upon the throne. What with road transport improving, the coming of the railway, the tightening up of the magistrates' courts, the appearance of the village constable, the game was not really worth the candle. It was something to look back upon with sighs and shakings of the head, the hard reality overshadowed and softened by the strange mythical charm that grows up about all dead and dying ventures, and the exploits of old people who once were young.

The smuggler of today, returning from a yachting cruise to the Continent with a few bottles of brandy concealed in his cabin locker, cuts a less romantic figure than the old-time fair-trader, his gesture rather a foolish fiddle to escape purchase-tax and spare his well-lined pocket. No Revenue cutters travel in his wake, or coast about offshore to bar his passage home. No warning shot passes across his bows to be answered by a twelve-pound gun, no boarding-parties, armed with sword and cutlass, demand surrender, to be met with a hot reception. Danger has gone. Punishment, if he is caught on arrival in port, means confiscation of his loot and a fine he is well able to pay. Customs officers, in mid-twentieth century, are after bigger fry – drug-pedlars at airports, diamond-thieves, gangs of inter-national crooks who will handle anything from heroin to Swiss watches.

The hundred inlets round the Cornish coast, with their once topical names whose origins are long-forgotten – Bessy's and Stack-house Cove, Brandy Cove and Lucky Hole – resound no longer to the stealthy crunch of a boat beaching at midnight, the low murmur of voices, and footsteps climbing the cliff-path. Holiday-makers picnic on the shore on summer days, children paddle in the pools and explore the empty caves. The mystery has gone.

On winter evenings, when a drifting mist makes all things silent and even mutes the sea, the shrouded outline of a humped rock above high-water, or a naked furze-bush clinging to the cliff's edge, seems, for a brief moment, to be a human form crouching in expectation of a signal. Phantom men people the coves, and whispers rise. Shadows are everywhere. Then a solitary black-backed gull utters a warning cry and dips to the sea. Nothing has changed, only the spirits and the ghosts have gone.

Chapter Fifteen

"THE WHERE AND WHEN"

WHAT does the future hold for Cornwall? Will it indeed become the playground of all England, chalets and holiday-camps set close to every headland, despite the efforts of the county planning authorities and the National Trust to preserve the coast? Pressure can be high from those bodies who see progress in every widened street, in every quayside cleared to allow more cars, more amusement arcades, more bingo-halls, bowling-alleys, dance-clubs, set upon sites where terraces or cottages once stood. The demand for these things exists, it is declared, and must be met. Cornwall depends upon the tourist, and if he does not find there the attractions of Blackpool or Southend he will no longer cross the Tamar, but take his custom somewhere else.

Those visitors who came to Cornwall in the past, year after year, because it offered a different sort of holiday, remote from the crowded seaside places, and with limited incomes were content to stay in farms, boarding houses, lodgings or quiet hotels, and explore the countryside and cliffs on foot, or picnic in the coves and on the once unlittered beaches without benefit of transistor, polythene packets and broken bottles, are forced, through disenchantment, to stay away. Nor is their presence missed.

Year by year the Cornish "playground" poses problems not reckoned upon when the trek south-west began. Cars, lined bumper to bumper, seek entry out of Devon into the peninsula, often held up for hours on their journey, and when they penetrate the narrower roads, many of them winding, with high hedgerows masking the view ahead, the driver, unused to the slower speed necessary when

Chalets and holiday-camps set close to every headland.

navigating these conditions, risks a head-on crash. He often gets it.

The sea around the Cornish coast, the north coast in particular, is dangerous at certain states of the tide. Surf-bathing has been a sport for many years, indulged in by all those who understand the hazards, but today the tourist who has learnt to swim a dozen strokes in his local swimming-bath ventures into the Atlantic rollers with total ignorance of their power, often disregarding the warning flag. Lifeguards upon the beaches do what they can, but a handful of trained men cannot watch hundreds of holiday-makers at the same time. Nor can harbour-masters, local boatmen, tug-skippers and others keep a weather eye open for every overcrowded boat that puts to sea in the charge of visitors incapable of handling their craft in anything but a flat calm.

The motorist who speeds along a Cornish lane at fifty miles an hour thinks he is competent to put his boat into a choppy sea at full-throttle, and is surprised when she is swamped or turns turtle. The lesson learnt, he decides to abandon the sea the next day, and climb the cliffs instead. Further misadventure follows. He is cut off by the rising tide, having forgotten to seek advice about the timing, and boldly starts upon a cliff-face that would daunt an experienced mountaineer in the high Alps. He is stuck, of course, halfway to the top, if he does not lose his head and crash to his death. Someone observes him from a distance. Coastguards are summoned, helicopters hover, a whole body of life-savers hurries to his rescue.

Cornwall, before it is turned into a playground, will have to legislate for those who refuse to be taught, and this is a delicate things to do *if* what the geese produce are golden eggs. The visitor with a real appreciation and respect for all he meets, from powerful seas and towering cliffs to windswept headlands and as yet uncluttered coves, would help to save these things he most enjoys if he would show himself more vocal in protest. A time will come when the mass invasion during the peak holiday season of August, with a lesser influx in June and July, can no longer be absorbed. Failure to house the wanderers who have not booked accommodation, a temporary breakdown in supplies bringing some measure of panic, freak weather of heat or rain sending people either to sleep upon the shores or to huddle in their cars, and the battle will be on. Not a fight between the unfortunate tourists, who will eventually find their way home, sadder and wiser than when they entered the peninsula, but between those who wish to preserve Cornwall for posterity and those who do not.

The hard truth is that the preservers are not always the indigenous, but too often sculptors, artists, writers, craftsmen, together with the elderly, the retired, the people who came to settle and put down roots; while their opponents, more recent newcomers, view the coast and countryside about them with a speculative eye. The Cornish people, their future and their way of life dependent upon what is to become of their county, are in the main indifferent to mushroom growth and change. The words progress, modernisation, go-ahead, have been sounded so often in their ears that they believe them to be synonymous with much that is hasty and ugly but beneficial to themselves. If this is how things are to be in the mid-twentieth century they feel they must adapt; the hard times of former years, when so many of their forebears were forced to emigrate, are not forgotten. Better to play host to the invaders, no matter in what capacity, providing a livelihood is gained, than pack up and start the race anew in another county where competition would be fiercer still.

That stalwart band of Cornish nationalists, Mebyon Kernow, would go to the other extreme and put the people into black kilts, speaking the old Cornish language, with a Parliament west of Tamar. The vision is idyllic but hardly practical. Invasion might be stemmed but men must live. If they would turn their genuine enthusiasm to seeking ways and means of preserving Cornish individuality and independence, keeping the coast and countryside unspoilt, with people fully employed, they might in time achieve a greater miracle than restoring a dead language that never, even in olden times, produced a living culture.

Writers, artists, actors do what they can to encourage interest in the arts, the spectacular open-air Minnack Theatre at Porthcurnow an example of their fervour. Groups in St. Ives, Newlyn and other centres, long or newly attached to their natural surroundings, give out, in good measure, what Cornwall first offered them by way of inspiration, but they must, by the very nature of their calling, stand apart from the main stream. Like Mebyon Kernow, the Sons of Cornwall, they are enthusiasts, driven to create, able to instruct or entertain according to their gifts, but are still persons in a minority, dedicated to the profession of their choice.

The counterblast to the mass invasion which leaves the county fallow for eight months of the year must surely come from a resurrection of those industries that once made Cornwall famous: tin-mining, quarrying, boat-building, fishing, engineering, china-clay working – the last two thriving, an inspiration to all who have the good fortune to be connected with their enterprise – together with other, newer industries for which the younger men and women could be trained. Motoring past Hayle with its generating station, old iron foundries and leaning cranes, and travelling north-eastward to the industrial lights of Camborne and Redruth, it is with a sense of

196

The spectacular open-air theatre at Porthcurnow.

wonder and excitement still to remember that Cornish commerce was born here, and that the landscape, however pitted it may be with sprawling villages and townships, unbeautiful and harsh, has been from the dawn of history the home of working men. Too often in the past, when the demand for tin fell and the mines sank into disuse, this was the scene of poverty and distress. Now, in the mid-1960s, hope has returned. Young men, whose fathers and grandfathers stood workless and dejected on the highway linking Camborne to Redruth, pour from the Camborne School of Mines or the engineering works of Holman Brothers, while gallant South Crofty Limited, at present one of the two surviving tin-mines, shows a greater increase in production and profit than it has done for sixty years.

What a triumph for ingenuity and modern planning, if in the next decade this matrix of Cornwall saw a great revival in the tin and copper trades, so that just as china-clay, further north, is shipped abroad from Par and Fowey, so the old mineral wealth, first heritage of Cornishmen, might be sought by markets throughout the world. It might even be possible for the encroaching sand in Hayle estuary to be defeated, stemmed, the channel deepened, and Hayle itself become a flourishing port once more.

This does not mean turning Cornwall into a Black Country full of belching chimneys, concrete factories and grey slums. Foresight and careful planning would be necessary, towns already in existence could be expanded and adapted for the purpose, giving work to the inhabitants already there. Architects with perception would be needed who would construct, or rebuild, those centres that too often in the early part of the present century suffered from the hands of men who had no eye for symmetry or grace.

The coast could still be spared, with the farmlands and the moors, and to preserve them for all time chosen areas could be declared a National Park. The high tors, the many miles of waste and lovely land, would be explored on horseback or on foot by those who have a taste for wilderness. Ornithologists, and seekers of wild flowers, would spend their leisure moments there; the young, and the old, who wish to test their stamina; the solitary, without any special bent or hobby, who are content simply to wander. These people and their pleasures, too often ignored in an age of rush and turmoil, would find in Cornwall's national park some measure of the peace they crave.

Another field of exploration, but by no means the least important (indeed, in days to come the findings might cover the whole peninsula), is among the barrows and tombs, the hidden villages, and – who knows? – perhaps the palaces and cities lying buried beneath the Cornish soil. Television can be thanked for the newly-awakened public interest in archaeology, and the diggers at Cadbury Hill in Somerset must not have it all their own way. The Arthur of legend covered many countries in his travels, the Arthur of history may yet be found, or rather his fortresses and dwellings, in Cornwall, Somerset and Wales.

Speculators who have hitherto sought profit in fun-fairs and amusement-arcades may care to sponsor an archaeological "dig" on promising ground. The result might warrant an extended search and a general reconstruction of the past in the levels laid bare. Who is to say there is no miniature Mycenae that has lain for over three thousand years beneath the grassland and the granite on the heights of West Penwith? No Minoan vessels sunk under the sands in Hayle estuary? No golden daggers and burnished swords beside the highway across Cornwall's backbone, and, long concealed within a cluster of tumbled stones above a moorland bog, a tiny figure of the Snake Goddess herself?

Fantasies, maybe, reminiscent of that uncle who sought for Shakespeare's manuscripts in the bed of the river Wye, but not impossible. Those Mediterranean peoples who travelled west and came upon the rugged Cornish coast, and braving the wild winter made their home upon its shores, are with us still, deep in the earth, amongst the mineral wealth they sought. What glory it would be if, by the year 2000, Cornwall had given the world not only new-found abundance of tin and copper, but the rich findings of an historical past hitherto unsuspected!

The Lost Land of Lyonesse may not be legendary, fathoms deep between the Scillies and Land's End, but may exist in truth beneath the soil we tread; yet even if no revelation comes, no sudden ring of spade upon stone upturning long-crumbled walls, the name itself can serve as metaphor, and inspiration to the Cornish young. This is their land, discovered long ago by men of courage, who brought with them the skills of a civilisation that has never been surpassed. These men were young also, for to travel uncharted seas in ancient days was not a pastime for the old, but a passion for exploration drove them out into mid-ocean and away from their own shores, and when they first looked upon the straggling Cornish coast, blue-watered then as now, rockbound, formidable, washed by seas reflecting a brighter sun than we know today, they may have thought they had circled their known world, and the land before them was another Minoan claw.

The drifting sands on which they beached their boats, the winding estuary, the narrow coves bare beneath the headland, covered all too swiftly by the fast-running tide, soon proved them wrong. Here was no familiar landfall but somewhere astonishing and strange, where the pale light lingered long after sundown, to be eclipsed, when the wind shifted, by a cloak of mist. They were not disconcerted but remained, or, like migrant birds, returned to their lands of origin to spread the news.

This hardy race of seamen and those who followed them, their zest for exploration burning still, hammered upon the rocks and broke the soil, creating, by their energy and courage, the Cornwall their successors knew, and know today.

This is Lyonesse, lost perhaps in legend but not in truth, waiting for other explorers, bred of the old stock, to found new legends and new skills. Cornwall is no lotus land for idle men, given up to dreams of vanished days, and hitherto the Cornish people have despised an easy way of life. Men who for centuries have known rock and gravel, sand and stone, do not always take easily to the factory floor, though when they do they apply their early cunning; while fishermen who used to sail offshore through the long winter nights, heedless of rising seas and driving rain, wear an uneasy look when steering a pleasure-boat in summer months, gunwale-down with tourists.

A great Cornishman, Arthur Quiller-Couch, the famous "Q," once wrote, "For my own part, as a Cornishman, I had rather preserve the old independent character of its sons; for it is unhappily certain that any people which lays itself out to exploit the stranger and the tourist runs a grave risk of deteriorating in manliness; and as I had rather be poor myself than subservient, so I would rather see my countrymen poor than subservient."

This was said over thirty years ago. Today, in the new age of scientific discovery and technological advance, poverty can and must be overcome. The challenge can be met, for the first invaders, when they settled amidst the scrub and granite to beget the Cornish race, bequeathed a legacy of tough endurance to their sons, an ability to withstand hardship, hunger, poverty and cold, and the will to overcome all four.

Some four centuries have passed since Cornishmen marched en masse across the Tamar in the Prayer Book Rebellion of 1549. Invasion has too often come from east to west. The last time the Cornish people threatened to cross the Tamar was during the reign of James II, when Bishop Jonathan Trelawny, of Trelawne in East Cornwall, was imprisoned in the Tower for protesting against the Declaration of Indulgence granting toleration to Catholics. The Bishop, an obstinate man, preferred to stand trial and possibly face execution rather than deny his principles; and his popularity was such that, although his fellow-Cornishmen did not care a jot about his principles, like Voltaire in another context they would fight to the death for his right to defend them. There was serious talk amongst some of them of marching to London and demanding Trelawny's release. "And shall Trelawny die?" became a catch-phrase throughout the county, with its echoing reply, "Here's twenty thousand Cornish men will know the reason why!"

Fortunately the necessity for the great march east never arose. Trewlawny was acquitted and released, and when William of Orange landed in England shortly afterwards Trelawny was one of his supporters, became Bishop of Exeter and later Winchester, and died, honoured and respected, in 1721, his body brought back to his native Pelynt for burial.

Few remember the strong-minded Bishop today, save for the hundreds of Cornish exiles who stamp and shout "The Song of the Western Men" when they gather together in South Africa, Australia, Canada, New Zealand and other countries far from home, to salute their county of origin. Trelawny, to the exiles, and to the Cornish of even a generation ago, was a symbol of defiance and solidarity. Parson Hawker, vicar of Morwenstow, composed the ballad, a rousing jingle if ever there was one, in Sir Bevil's Walk in Stowe Wood, a most suitable spot for inspiration. If successive governments continue to ignore Cornwall's demand for assistance and investment in an industrial revival we may see another rebellion yet, with invasion taking place from west to east.

> "And have they fix'd the where and when?
>   And shall Trelawny die?
>   Here's twenty thousand Cornish men
>   Will know the reason why!
>
> "We'll cross the Tamar, land to land;
>   The Severn is no stay;
>   With 'one and all' and hand in hand,
>   And who shall bid us nay?
>
> "And when we come to London Wall,
>   A pleasant sight to view,
>   Come forth! Come forth, ye cowards all,
>   Here's men as good as you!
>
> "Trelawny he's in keep and hold;
>   Trelawny he may die;
>   But here's twenty thousand Cornish men,
>   Will know the reason why!"

The population of Cornwall today is some 342,000 strong. Treasure still lies beneath the Cornish soil awaiting harvest, and although the

Mediterranean dust has long lain scattered on the Cornish hills, merging with slate and shale, something remains, particles unfelt, unseen, coursing through the blood, directing impulse. The challenge is to the young.

Epilogue

THIRTEEN years have passed since my son and I explored the county together, he taking the black-and-white photographs and I, with the help of research and my own memories, preparing to write *Vanishing Cornwall*. The book was published a year later, and, I am happy to say, found favour not only with the Cornish people but with others, who came from various parts of the United Kingdom as well as from overseas. My son is an explorer still, and has taken many beautiful coloured photographs in place of the original black-and-white, but I must confess that this time, being thirteen years older and in my early seventies, my enthusiasm for wandering has vanished, like much of the Cornwall that I knew.

History cannot change, nor the sea, nor the varying contours of the land, nor the spirit of the people; but those readers who now follow the original text, as they turn the pages of the book or wander forth to seek the places I have described, are bound to find certain alterations. This epilogue is for them.

Already, though, I write in error. The sea *can* change, and the contours of the land. Par Bay, once milky white from the streams that fed it, is too often now a turbid brown, whether from drains or oil-polluted seaweed – who can say? I only know that when I walk the strand there with my dogs the stench appals me and the people who live near by, although the many visitors who come to swim seem undeterred. The contours of the land, the mountain peaks of china clay I liked to think of as a lunar landscape, they too have altered. Environmentalists considered them ugly. So they are now half their original size and flat on top, some of them not even white. Perhaps it was my eye that was at fault in finding the peaks beautiful. But at least the china-clay industry flourishes, which is what matters most.

The spirit of the local people here about me does not change, and, having lived in Cornwall now for more than fifty years, I can laugh with them when they talk of "emmets", the Cornish word for strangers. Too many houses, bungalows, cottages which they could live in themselves are let at vast sums to summer visitors. Somebody benefits, but exactly who I never can discover. The Tourist Board, perhaps. More caravans, more chalets, every year . . . But enough of this.

The National Trust does fine work in helping to preserve the coast, and the cliffs, and many of the larger houses that were once the homes of the gentry described in the text of *Vanishing Cornwall*. Lanhydrock is one of these: splendidly preserved, house and gardens, and well worth visiting. Other smaller properties come to mind, which are privately owned though also on view, but in the text I made something of a feature of the rectory at Warleggan, which appeared so haunting, and is now turned into flats, with the strange rector, let us hope, content and now at rest.

The tin-mines, I am glad to report, have had a revival. Wheal Jane and Wellington were working in this year of 1979, though flooding has been a possibility. Fishing is also much to the fore, with mackerel the main objective. Unfortunately, big trawlers from the north, French trawlers from the south, and Russian factory-ships now haunt the southern coast of Cornwall, netting the fish that belongs by right to Cornish fishermen.

Here is something that the Cornish nationalists – who split from Mebyon Kernow, mentioned in the chapter "Where and When" – might take up as a challenge, and be supported by all who live in the county. Otherwise their movement is something of a puzzle. Like the Scots, the Welsh, the Bretons and the Basques, they believe in Cornwall for the Cornish. But, in 1979, who exactly are the Cornish people? Those who were born and bred here, and can legitimately claim Cornish descent through both parents and grandparents, yes indeed. But how many of them are there? Precious few, compared with those who have married and intermarried with men and women from other counties, and are therefore not pure-bred. May they speak and read in Cornish, if they wish, but how they would live and be independent financially from England across the Tamar they do not say, as yet.

What of smuggling, or fair-traders, as I call them in this book? If fair-trading in 1979 means the crunch of boats beaching at dawn or even at mid-day in Talland Bay, laden with the unlawful heroin and possibly other forbidden drugs, it continues still, to the detriment of all, Cornish and English alike.

Finally, to return to myself, as author of the book, and to the unchanged text. When I wrote it, in 1966, I lived at Menabilly, a happy tenant. Now I am equally content at Kilmarth, the one-time dower house, with my landlord, Philip Rashleigh and his wife, dear and good neighbours in their rightful home of Menabilly.

My husband's boat *Ygdrasil*, "poor Yggy", as he called her latterly, stands here at Kilmarth, in what was once an orchard, rather the worse for weather and for wear, but a playground for our grand-children, and none of us has so far vanished.

Whether this site was truly the last outpost of an aged Cornish King – King Mark – is still unproven. Research showed me that a Roger Kylmerth lived here in 1327, and his name could have derived from the words Retreat of Mark. Equally, in Cornish, it can mean a grove for horses! The cattle and the sheep graze happily beyond the hedge, but so far not a horse in sight. In the past, perhaps. In the future, who can say?

The challenge is still to the young.

Kilmarth
1980

Bibliography

Survey of Cornwall by Robert Morden. Approx. 1712.

Parochial History of Cornwall, 1868. Published William Lake, Truro, and John Camden Hotten, London.

Cornwall. A Survey. Prepared by W. Harding Thompson, F.R.I.B.A., for the Cornwall Branch of the Council for the Preservation of Rural England. 1930. Pub. University of London Press.

A History of Cornwall by F. E. Halliday. 1959. Pub. Duckworth & Co. Ltd., London.

Essays in Cornish History by Charles Henderson. 1935. Pub. Clarendon Press, Oxford.

A Londoner's Walk to the Land's End by Walter White. 1865. Pub. Chapman and Hall, London.

Cornwall and Its Coasts by Alphonse Esquiros. 1865. Pub. Chapman and Hall, London.

Rambles Beyond Railways by Wilkie Collins. 1861. Pub. Richard Bentley, London.

Traditions and Hearthside Stories of West Cornwall by William Bottrell. 1870. Pub. Beare & Sons, Penzance.

History of Polperro by Jonathan Couch. 1871. Pub. W. Lake, Truro.

Ancient and Holy Wells of Cornwall by M. & L. Quiller-Couch. 1894. Pub. Clark, London.

The Cornish Miner by A. K. Hamilton Jenkin. 1927. Pub. Allen & Unwin, London.

The Story of Cornwall by A. K. Hamilton Jenkin. 1934. Pub. George Nelson & Sons, London.

Days in Cornwall by C. Lewis Hind. 1907. Pub. Methuen & Co., London.

Black's *Guide to Cornwall.* 1892. Pub. Adam & Charles Black, London and Edinburgh.

Cornwall. A Shell Guide by John Betjeman. 1964. Pub. Faber and Faber, London.

A Glossary of Cornish Names by the Rev. John Bannister, LL.D. 1871. Pub. Williams & Norgate, London.

An English-Cornish Dictionary by R. Moreton Nance. 1952. Pub. Worden (Printers), Penzance.

The Mines and Mineral Railways of East Cornwall and West Devon by D. B. Barton. 1964. Truro Bookshop.

A History of Copper Mining in Cornwall by D. B. Barton. 1961. Truro Bookshop.

Journals of the Royal Institution of Cornwall (various). Oscar Blackford Ltd., Truro.